Prescribing Justice

A Doctor's Fight for Truth

For permission requests, please contact the publisher at:
Quiet Minds, Inc.
12955 Biscayne Blvd, Suite 320
North Miami, Florida 33181
www.prescribingjustice.com
info@prescribingjustice.com

Library of Congress Cataloging-in-Publication Data:
Poitier Jr, MD, Joseph and Pierce, Deanna
Prescribing Justice: A Doctor's Fight for Truth
979-8-3294804-0-5

Editors: Joseph Poitier Jr., MD and Deanna Pierce
Proofreader: ProofreadingPal
Typist: Sue Smith

Artwork by Deanna Pierce and creative initiation with the assistance of Pecan Tree Publishing.

The pictures in this book are from the pre-digital era. Just as vinyl records offer no options for autotune, many of these photos are vintage. We are simply delighted to have them and be able to share them with you. Respect our Kodak throwbacks.

The information in this book is for general informational purposes only. The authors and publisher make no representations or warranties, express or implied, about the completeness, accuracy, reliability, suitability, or availability of the information for any purpose. Any reliance you place on such information is strictly at your own risk.

Dedication

To my beloved family, who have stood by me with unwavering support and boundless love throughout every twist and turn of this remarkable journey. Your presence has been my greatest blessing, grounding me in moments of doubt and lifting me to new heights of achievement.

To my patients, whose stories of resilience and courage have left an indelible mark on my heart. Your trust in my care has been a profound honor, driving me to strive for excellence in every interaction. It is your strength in the face of adversity that fuels my commitment to providing compassionate, equitable health care for all.

And to every individual who has ever felt marginalized or overlooked within our health-care system, particularly Black men and minorities who bear the brunt of systemic disparities and injustices: your struggles are not unnoticed, your voices are not unheard. May this book serve as a beacon of hope and empowerment, a testament to our shared determination to break down barriers and build a future where every individual receives the quality care they deserve.

In the name of progress, equality, and the unending pursuit of justice, I dedicate these pages to you. May they inspire change, spark conversation, and pave the way for a brighter, more inclusive tomorrow.

~Joseph Poitier Jr., MD

The Poitier family in a 2007 file photo taken in Atlanta. From left: Alexandria Poitier, Bernadette Poitier, Dr. Joseph Poitier Jr., Sidney Poitier, Joni Poitier, and Arleen Poitier.

Acknowledgments

This book is written on behalf of all the men and women who are incarcerated for no reason other than being mentally ill.

May they all one day be free.

Dr. Joseph and Josephine Poitier Sr., without whom I would not be here.

Mr. Hayward and Mrs. Corine Lofton, without whom I would not have my wife, Arleen.

Dr. Alexandria Poitier and Attorney Joni Poitier, my children. My sister, Bernadette Poitier, who has been my supportive and near twin throughout my life.

All my friends who worked in the jail, who are too numerous to name, but some will be: Theodore Thomas, Carter Wiggins, Allen Monica, all the officers and members of the mental health team and medical teams at the Miami-Dade County jail. The Grand Dame of Black mental health in Miami, Dr. Evalina Bestman.

My CEO, Michele Sweeting.

To my best friends who happen to be psychiatrists: Dr. Ethel Andrews and Dr. Allen Singer.

My elementary school teachers at Holy Redeemer Catholic School: Sister Mary Clementina and Mrs. Iona Strachan. My high school teachers.

My college instructors: Dr. Henry Cecil McBay, Dr. Frederick E. Mapp, and Dr. Tom Norris.

My medical school instructors: Dr. Robert Cahill and Dr. Vincent Ziboh, with whom I spent summers in his research lab.

My psychiatric instructors: Dr. Richard Steinbook, Dr. Barry Morris, Dr. Sanford Jacobson, Dr. Lloyd Miller, and Dr. Charles Mutter.

Dr. Robert Bragg, former Professor of Psychiatry at the University of Miami, deserves special thanks for mentoring many Black students at the University of Miami Miller School of Medicine.

Corporal Barney, whose friendship, tenacity, brilliance, and brotherhood helped to set me free.

Thank GOD for the cameras and tapes.

To our brothers behind bars,
You are not forgotten. We are tirelessly striving to create change,
and you are at the heart of our efforts. You are in our prayers, in
our thoughts, and you are our daily inspiration to continue fighting
the good fight. Stay strong, as we continue this journey together.

Table of Contents

"Fragmented Strength" by Deanna Pierce, 2024

Foreword

In the pages that follow, we will embark on a journey that explores the intricate web of societal prejudices and systemic injustices that intersect within the corridors of our nation's jails. Through the lens of one man's experience, we are compelled to confront uncomfortable truths about race, incarceration, and the power structures that shape our criminal justice system.

This narrative challenges us to acknowledge our assumptions and biases, urging us to peel back the layers of complacency and indifference that too often shield us from the harsh realities faced by marginalized communities. As we delve into the depths of this story, let us not avert our gaze from the stark inequalities that continue to plague our society, but instead, let us tackle them head-on with courage and conviction. As we pause and reflect on the complexities of this story, we are reminded of our collective responsibility to dismantle the structures of oppression and to strive for a society where justice is truly blind and equitable for all.

Let us begin with open hearts and minds, ready to accept uncomfortable truths and to champion the cause of justice. Together may we forge a path toward a future where every individual, regardless of race or background, can live with dignity, freedom, and the promise of a brighter tomorrow.

I hope this book will serve as a clarion call for change, inspiring us all to strive for a more just and equitable world where every individual, regardless of race or circumstance, is afforded the dignity and respect they deserve.

Preface

Preface has been written by Pete Earley Author of CRAZY:
A Father's Search Through America's Mental Health Madness,
one of two finalists for the 2007 Pulitzer Prize.

Dr. Joseph Poitier Jr. is an uncommon man.

Few psychiatrists choose to treat the seriously mentally ill. They prefer to help the "worried well," individuals with good insurance plans who have difficulties in their lives coping with relationships or unpleasant circumstances. Those with the cruelest mental illnesses, such as schizophrenia (1% of Americans) and bipolar 1 (2.8% of the population), are extremely challenging to help, often poor, and unstable.

Beginning in the 1960s with the massive shuttering of state-run mental hospitals, the sickest of the sick were discharged with little or no support. Many ended up in substandard assisted living facilities, others became homeless on our streets and still others were locked up in jails and prisons. Tragically, that horrific trend continues today.

As I write this, more than 365,000 Americans with serious mental illnesses are incarcerated. Each year, 2.3 million are booked into our jails. One million are on probation. Studies have shown that 40 percent of seriously mentally ill individuals will have a dangerous encounter with law enforcement during their lifetimes. They are 16 times more likely to be fatally shot by the police. They will stay in jails and prisons four-to-eight times longer than others charged with identical crimes. They face a higher likelihood of having additional charges pressed against them while they are in custody. They cost seven times as much to imprison and they have a recidivism rate that is 15% higher than the national average. Some 85% will return to jails after they are first arrested. Finally, they will die 15 to 20 years before others their age. They are "faceless and nameless, lost in plain sight, and forced to live on the fringes of society," Howard K. Koh, M.D. has noted.

If society's neglect is not enough, their illnesses torture them even more. "It must be remembered that for the person with severe mental illness who has no treatment, the most dreaded of confinements can be the imprisonment inflicted by his own mind, which shuts reality out and subjects him to the torment of voices and images beyond our powers to describe," U.S. Supreme Court Justice Anthony M. Kennedy wrote.

If you visit any jail or prison in America, you will reach another deeply disturbing realization. Most of the seriously mentally ill in custody are poor and black.

These unfortunate individuals are who Dr. Poitier has dedicated his career to helping. I first met him when I arrived outside the Miami-Dade Pretrial Detention Center in the heart of Miami while doing research in 2004 for a nonfiction book about the criminalization of individuals with mental illnesses. I had been turned away from jails in Los Angeles, Chicago, New York, Baltimore and Washington D.C., because officials didn't want me to see the awful conditions there. But a reform minded Miami judge, the Honorable Steven Leifman, arranged for me to have unlimited access at the Miami detention center. Dr. Poitier was my guide. At the time, the jail held 1,712 prisoners. It was estimated that 16 to 20 percent had a diagnosed serious mental illness. You can do the math. Dr.

Poitier was the jail's only doctor charged with helping more than 300 patients daily. The ninth floor was where the most suicidal and delusional were housed. Dr. Poitier warned me when I first arrived that what I was about to observe was "unconscionable." Even so, I was not prepared for what I witnessed when I entered that cell block the first time.

The stench of urine and antiseptic burned my nostrils. Cells meant to hold two men, held four or more. Nearly all prisoners were naked. Plexiglass that had been installed on cell bars to prevent inmates from throwing urine and feces at correctional officers blocked the air conditioning vents, turning cells into ice boxes. Some days, there was no running water. Inmates, thirsty because of medication, drank from toilets. None of the guards assigned to the ninth floor had received any specialized training to handle the mentally ill. They begrudgingly called this the "forgotten floor." It was not only because of the inmates housed there. Most of the officers assigned to work on the cellblock were being punished by their superiors. One correctional officer was openly known for beating prisoners and when I confronted him, he explained, unapologetically that "even a crazy man listens to fists." One particular image is burned into my memory. A big African American prisoner accused of trespassing (a common nuisance charge used by businesses to get a mentally impaired individual off the street) stood naked in his cell so ill that he could not speak. His eyes stared forward without emotion. He grunted and the officers controlled him by giving him sandwiches. He was soon released only to return two days later.

This was the "unconscionable" world that Dr. Poitier entered by choice. For ten months, I watched him day-in-and-day-out making his rounds, stopping outside each cell (there was no privacy) doing his best to evaluate, diagnose and help each inmate, knowing that some would be released to the streets before the medication that he prescribed would have time to help, knowing that others would get new, more serious charges (usually assaulting an officer) and would be shipped off to prison and further denigration. He recognized the regulars as they cycled through a revolving door, forever entangled in a system designed for punishment not for healing. And yet, he made his rounds without pause, listening to each inmate, quietly determined to do what he could to help them.

There were good reasons why other psychiatrists avoided what Dr. Poitier so willingly elected to do and yet, the only complaints that I ever heard him utter were about the need for more humane treatment options. It was not only his medical skills that helped those during his rounds, but something more. Dr. Poitier genuinely cared about these men and, I believe, part of his ability to form an instant connection came from his own past and the racism that he'd faced as a black man becoming a psychiatrist.

This is why I am thrilled that Dr. Poitier is now chronicling his experiences. This book is an expose that reveals the barbarity of what has happened and continues to happen in too many jails and prisons today. It is a story that can only be told by only someone who has been a doctor on a "ninth floor" and who personally witnessed the inhumanity such places breed.

But there is a larger tale within these pages. This is a story about one man's determination, courage and compassion. It is the story of a doctor who showed me the best of his profession, a healer who not only used his medical skills to help society's throw-away people, but who gave those in the jail hope by showing them that he cared and that their lives mattered. When I first met him outside the Miami jail, Dr. Poitier was waging a campaign for reform. He still is fighting that battle. And the men's lives he touched were better because of him. The question is whether we are listening.

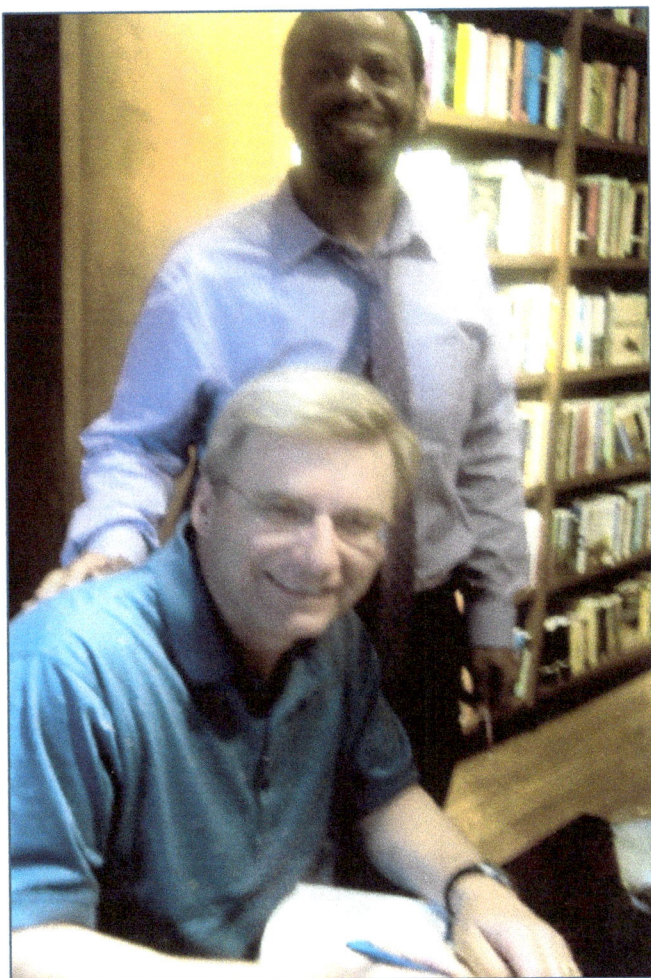

Author Pete Earley and Dr. Joseph Poitier, Jr.

Chapter 1: Denied Entry

"Justice delayed is justice denied"—a common tenet in the legal domain. These words originated from my fellow alumnus, the Reverend Dr. Martin Luther King Jr. We both graduated from Morehouse College. The school is known as a "Candle in the Dark" because there is an expectation that every graduate will leave an indelible mark in attempting to cure the ills of society. What you will read in this book is one man's attempt to fulfill this mission.

"Reverend Martyr King" by Deanna Pierce, 2024

It all started with me, a Black psychiatrist, being denied entrance into the Miami-Dade County Jail System. This facility embodies one of the most discriminatory institutions in this country - the criminal justice system. I was denied entrance to a place overrepresented by the poor, minorities, and the uneducated (particularly Black and Hispanic). I was not the perpetrator. In fact, in many ways, I attempted to be a

1

champion But thousands of mentally ill individuals, primarily Black and Hispanic but also White, were caught up in the system not designed for them. It was not designed for them because most of the incarcerated in our jail and prison system suffer from mental illness.

Like Moses, I wanted to lead this incarcerated population to a promised land—a promised land of mental freedom. I sought to help those who were wallowing in the throes of mental discord due to abnormalities in their brain functioning. I sought to rid the jails of those who should have been hospitalized rather than face the harshness of a jail system designed for criminals. But that was not to be.

Aspersions were cast against prescribed best-practice professional efforts, just as they have been against men of courage in the past. Despite numerous successful years of working to take care of those who suffer from major mental disorders—such as schizophrenia, depression, bipolar disorder, and substance abuse—my name and work were defamed.

It is easy for most Black men to be incarcerated. A Pew study in May of 2023, collecting data from 595 jails—showed that Blacks made up 12% of the local population, but 26% of the jail population. The study showed that in 26% of jails, the share of Black inmates was more than twice their share in the community. In 29% of jails, that share was four times their share in the community.

The American Civil Liberties Union (ACLU) published a study in 2018, which was done by several members of the University of Miami's Department of Sociology, which revealed the racial disparities in our criminal justice system: "Unequal Treatment: Racial and Ethnic Disparities in the Dade County Criminal Justice System."

A little-known fact is that those treated unfairly often suffer from mental illness, with the unfortunate reality that a majority of these individuals are Black. Within these pages, you will delve into the journey of one Black man's endeavor to rectify injustices in mental health care. Although his efforts were commendable, those he sought to help were often devastated when economic circumstances took a downturn. There's a saying that when White people catch the flu, Black people catch pneumonia. This narrative encapsulates his personal battle against a system that has shattered countless lives. It stands as a testament to the unquestioning support of his loved ones and his commitment to upholding justice for those grappling with mental illness, which commitment has kept him alive long enough to pen these words.

You have been told where the exact data can be found. What you'll read in this book is a first-hand account of what went on in the Miami-Dade County jail system and what goes on in many other jail systems throughout this country. It is a sad story, a story about the persecution of the just and a failure of local communities, states, and this country to address the problems of the chronically mentally ill. It also highlights the need to produce more Black mental health professionals, including psychiatrists, psychologists, social workers, and licensed mental health counselors.

So let us explore why they wouldn't let this Black man in the jail.

Our criminal justice system bears the indelible mark of racial inequity, disproportionately ensnaring individuals of Black and Brown descent. I disdain the narrow label "African American" in favor of the broader, more inclusive terms "Black and Brown," acknowledging the wide spectrum of identities within these communities. Indeed, skin color does not dictate one's heritage nor define their struggles.

It is a damning reality that Black and Brown men form the backbone of our incarcerated population, a testament to the systemic injustices embedded in our society. What is perhaps most chilling is the youth of those affected, their potential squandered behind bars during what should be their most vibrant years. They are often born into poverty, navigating a labyrinth of disadvantage with little hope of escape.

The origins of this crisis trace back to the darkest chapters of our history—slavery and the enduring legacy of racism. Countless scholarly works have dissected this festering wound, among them Slavery by Another Name written by Douglas A. Blackmon and The New Jim Crow written by Michelle Alexander. These texts serve as powerful indictments of a system that perpetuates cycles of oppression, echoing the ghosts of past injustices.

In echoing Michelle Alexander's heart-rending observations, we confront a disconcerting truth: our purported stronghold of justice bears an unsettling resemblance to its antithesis, slavery. The marginalized and disenfranchised are left to deteriorate, their voices drowned out by the disharmony of privilege. Financial barriers further entrench this divide, rendering justice a commodity truly accessible only to the affluent.

As we confront this harrowing reality, we must ask ourselves: How can a nation founded on principles of equality reconcile with a justice system so fundamentally unequal? What will it take to dismantle the shackles of oppression that continue to bind generations of Black and Brown lives? These are not just questions of policy but of morality, demanding introspection, and action from each of us. For until justice truly becomes blind to skin color, our society will remain shackled to its past, unable to attain its full potential.

"Prisons and jails do not disappear social problems. They disappear human beings. Homelessness, unemployment, drug

4

addiction, mental illness and illiteracy are only a few of the problems that disappear from public view when the human beings entering with them are relegated to cages." Angela Davis, political activist, scholar, and author.

Many laws enacted in the 1980s in an attempt to get tough on crime and curb the drug epidemic led to excess incarceration of many men and women of color. Scientific studies since then have shown that most substance abuse problems are actually brain-based. There are treatments for many substance abuse disorders such as alcoholism and opioid abuse. A relatively new drug, Suboxone, has been a miracle wonder for opioid and fentanyl abusers. It allows those with opioid abuse disorders to transform into working human beings without appearing ill.

Patients in methadone clinics often have distinctive physical characteristics that set them apart from others that is a frightening and disheartening look. With Suboxone, former users can lead complete lives, return to work, get their degrees, and function in society as normal human beings. It is indeed a miracle drug, but one must have faith and a belief in science. Those with substance abuse disorders must also have a belief in themselves and that their illness can indeed be placed in remission. They must have caretakers who believe in them as well and are willing to prescribe these new modern medications, which are totally life altering.

In the past, access to treatments for mental health and substance abuse disorders was often limited for Black and Brown inmates due to various systemic barriers. These barriers included disparities in health-care access, economic inequalities, and discriminatory practices. As a result, many people from marginalized communities faced significant challenges in obtaining the care they desperately needed.

However, in recent years, there has been a notable shift in the availability and accessibility of these treatments. Thanks to efforts aimed at addressing health-care disparities and increasing access to mental health and substance abuse services, treatments that were once out of reach are now much more accessible.

One significant change has been the expansion of services to local communities. Instead of having to travel long distances to specialized facilities, individuals can now access treatment closer to home. Local drug stores and community clinics have become important hubs for mental health and substance abuse services. This proximity not only reduces logistical barriers but also helps integrate mental health and substance abuse treatment into primary care settings, making it easier to seek help.

Additionally, awareness campaigns and outreach efforts have been instrumental in informing communities about available resources. Community organizations, health-care providers, and government agencies have worked together to spread awareness about the importance of seeking help for mental health and substance abuse issues. By reducing stigma and increasing education about available treatments, these initiatives have helped empower patients to seek the care they need.

Furthermore, policy changes have played a crucial role in expanding access to treatment. Initiatives aimed at increasing insurance coverage for mental health and substance abuse services have made it more affordable for individuals to access treatment. Medicaid expansion in many states has also widened the safety net for those who previously lacked insurance coverage, particularly among low-income and marginalized communities.

Overall, these changes represent significant progress in addressing disparities in treatment access. By making treatments more accessible and integrating them into local communities, more Black and Brown people can now receive the care they need to overcome mental health and substance abuse challenges.

"Problem-solving courts" are now flourishing in some states. These courts are designed to aid those who have mental health challenges, substance abuse problems, and disorders that may have been triggered from military service. Problem-solving courts are now the standard of justice and therapeutic jurisprudence in our criminal justice system. Such courts look to rehabilitate rather than punish. They take care of people who have serious mental disorders, those who have problems with domestic violence, and those who suffer from substance abuse disorders.

Several years ago, I read Therapeutic Jurisprudence: The Law as a Therapeutic Agent, a 1990 book by David B. Wexler. It aroused my interest in treatment rather than punishment of those who suffered from mental or substance abuse disorders or of those who had relationship problems.

The term "therapeutic jurisprudence" (TJ) was coined by Wexler, a professor at the University of Arizona Rogers College of Law and the University of Puerto Rico School of Law in a paper presented to the National Institute of Mental Health in 1987. Alongside Professor Bruce Winick of the University of Miami School of Law, Wexler developed this new perspective to examine how substantive rules, legal procedures, and the actions of legal actors (primarily lawyers and judges) influence the therapeutic or antitherapeutic outcomes for those involved in the legal process.

In the early 1990s, legal scholars began to explore TJ, initially focusing on Wexler's 1990 book and on Wexler and Winick's subsequent 1991 book, Essays in Therapeutic Jurisprudence, both of which contributed significantly to the establishment of TJ as a framework for understanding the psychological impact of legal processes. Professor Winick also held a faculty appointment in the Department of Psychiatry at the University of Miami. He was a brilliant man whom I had the opportunity to observe lecture about mental health and the law.

Over time, the TJ approach expanded beyond mental health law to encompass various areas, including criminal law, family and juvenile law, health law, tort law, contracts and commercial law, trusts and estates law, disability law, constitutional law, evidence law, and the legal profession as a whole. TJ emerged as a comprehensive approach to law, focusing on promoting psychological well-being and reducing unintended negative consequences for individuals interacting with the legal system.

One significant application of TJ was in the development of problem-solving courts, such as drug treatment courts (DTCs), mental health courts, domestic violence courts, reentry courts, teen courts, and community courts. These courts, informed by the principles of TJ, aim to address underlying issues and to promote rehabilitation rather than solely focusing on punishment.

While the TJ movement originated in the United States, it gained traction in countries such as Canada, Australia, and New Zealand. More recently, TJ concepts have been integrated into legal systems worldwide, including in Israel, Pakistan, India, and Japan. The establishment of the International Society for Therapeutic Jurisprudence reflects the growing international recognition and adoption of TJ principles.

TJ represents a paradigm shift in the legal field, emphasizing the importance of promoting well-being and addressing underlying issues. By embracing TJ principles, legal systems can move toward a more compassionate and effective approach to justice, focusing on rehabilitation and support rather than punishment alone.

Our criminal justice system is overrun by people who are poor and uninformed, frequently having bad or absent role models who may cause them to view incarceration or imprisonment as a sign of power and strength. Little do they know that a felony record strips certain citizenship rights including job access, one's ability to vote, one's ability to serve on a jury, the access to financial aid for education purposes, and even the ability to seek housing assistance or financing.

Yes, some of our judges and judicial systems have become enlightened. This is a far cry from my first time in court pleading with a judge to get someone who had been hospitalized an involuntarily injectable medication. I was practically laughed out of court without cause. The judge had my patient come and stand at his side and mocked me in my attempts to get him the proper treatment. The judge was a former pharmacist; he asked me if I had ever seen the movie, One Flew Over the Cuckoo's Nest.

The judge's ignorance of mental health treatment resulted in a mockery of the court proceedings and had serious consequences for the defendant. Due to this lack of understanding, the defendant was unjustly kept in a mental institution for an extended time without receiving the appropriate treatment he desperately needed.

We later returned to the same courtroom, where a more enlightened judge gave us the treatment order we were seeking, which was in accord with Chapter 916 of the Florida statutes. To this day, I try to forget the ordeal. This young man was a Black man who was obviously not well, even to a nonprofessional.

That experience underscores the importance of having judges who are well-informed about mental health issues and treatment options within the criminal justice system. By ensuring that legal professionals have a thorough understanding of mental health matters, we can prevent injustices and ensure that individuals receive the appropriate care and support they need to overcome their challenges.

The stark reality is that Black men constitute nearly 67 percent of the current population in prison or on probation. Lesser known, particularly to their family members, is that a significant portion (around 60 to 70 percent) of those behind bars also grapple with some form of mental illness. These illnesses are not synonymous with criminal behavior; rather, they often stem from underlying brain dysfunction.

Comparing the body to a vehicle, if the heart serves as the engine that keeps us alive, then the brain acts as the transmission that enables us to function. Mental illnesses, much like physical ailments, can impair cognitive function, emotional regulation, and decision-making processes. When untreated, these conditions can exacerbate social and behavioral challenges, sometimes leading people into the criminal justice system.

It is crucial to recognize that mental illness knows no bounds of race or ethnicity. However, systemic inequities and socioeconomic disparities disproportionately impact marginalized communities, including the Black community, exacerbating their vulnerability to mental health challenges. Moreover, systemic racism often perpetuates cycles of incarceration rather than addressing underlying mental health needs.

Acknowledging the prevalence of mental illness among the incarcerated is a critical step in understanding the multifaceted dynamics at play. It is essential to recognize that mental health issues often intersect with systemic factors such as poverty, trauma, discrimination, and lack of access to quality health care. This complex interplay contributes to the overrepresentation of individuals with mental illness in jails.

By addressing the root causes of mental health disparities and systemic inequalities, we can begin to dismantle the pathways that lead individuals into the criminal justice system. This requires a comprehensive approach that prioritizes mental health treatment and support services both inside correctional facilities and in communities
at large.

Within correctional settings, it is imperative to provide access to evidence-based mental health interventions, including therapy, medication, and peer support programs. Correctional staff should receive training in recognizing and responding to mental health crises, and specialized mental health units should be established to provide intensive care for individuals with severe psychiatric disorders.

Additionally, reentry programs should be implemented to support those with mental illness as they transition back into the community. This includes providing access to housing, employment, education, and health-care services that are tailored to meet their unique needs. By addressing the social determinants of health and promoting community integration, we can reduce the likelihood of individuals with mental illness becoming re-involved in the criminal justice system.

Expanding mental health services beyond correctional facilities is paramount to addressing the underlying issues contributing to incarceration rates. One crucial step is to increase access to mental health clinics, ensuring that people have a safe and supportive environment to seek treatment and support. These clinics should offer a range of services, including counseling, therapy, medication management, and case management, tailored to the specific needs of each person.

Additionally, crisis intervention teams play a vital role in de-escalating mental health crises in the community. These teams, comprising mental health professionals and law enforcement officers trained in crisis intervention techniques, can provide immediate support and connect individuals in crisis with appropriate resources and services. By diverting such people away from the criminal justice system and toward mental health treatment, crisis intervention teams can help prevent unnecessary incarceration and promote recovery.

Supportive housing programs are another critical component of community-based mental health services. These programs provide stable and affordable housing to the mentally ill, along with access to on-site support services such as counseling, case management, and life-skills training. By addressing housing needs, supportive housing programs help create a foundation for stability and recovery, reducing the likelihood of involvement with the criminal justice system.

Empowering community-based organizations to provide culturally competent and linguistically appropriate services is essential for ensuring that mental health services are accessible to those from diverse backgrounds. These organizations can play a pivotal role in reaching underserved communities, offering services that are sensitive to cultural beliefs, values, and practices. By fostering partnerships between mental health providers and community organizations, we can create a network of support that meets the unique needs of all, regardless of their background or circumstances.

In summary, investing in mental health services in the community is essential for addressing the root causes of incarceration and promoting recovery and well-being. By expanding access to mental health clinics, crisis intervention teams, supportive housing programs, and culturally competent services, we can create a more equitable and compassionate system of care that supports individuals on their journey to healing and recovery.

Reducing the stigma surrounding mental illness and promoting help-seeking behavior are essential steps in creating a more supportive and compassionate society. Stigma often prevents individuals from seeking the help they need, leading to delayed treatment, increased suffering, and, in some cases, involvement with the criminal justice system. Efforts to combat stigma and encourage help-seeking behavior can have a profound impact on well-being and community resilience.

One approach to reducing stigma is through education and awareness campaigns that provide accurate information about mental health issues. These campaigns can help dispel myths and misconceptions about mental illness, fostering a more informed and empathetic understanding of the challenges of living with mental health conditions. By raising awareness about the prevalence of mental illness and its impact on individuals, families, and communities, we can create a more supportive environment that encourages open dialogue and acceptance.

In addition to education and awareness, it is crucial to promote positive portrayals of mental illness in the media and popular culture. By highlighting stories of recovery, resilience, and empowerment, we can challenge negative stereotypes and offer hope to those struggling with mental health issues. Media campaigns, documentaries, and storytelling initiatives can all play a role in shifting public perceptions and attitudes toward mental illness, encouraging empathy, and understanding.

Furthermore, destigmatizing mental illness requires the active involvement of community leaders, health-care professionals, and policymakers. By advocating for policies and initiatives that support mental health awareness and access to care, we can create a more inclusive and supportive society for those living with mental illness. This may include funding for mental health programs, expansion of mental health services, and integration of mental health education into school curricula.

Ultimately, reducing stigma surrounding mental illness is a collective effort that requires the commitment and engagement of people, communities, and institutions. By promoting awareness, challenging stereotypes, and advocating for change, we can create a more compassionate society where everyone feels valued, supported, and empowered to seek help when needed.

Breaking the cycles of incarceration and promoting rehabilitation and healing necessitates a comprehensive and collaborative approach that tackles the root causes of mental health disparities and systemic inequalities. Prioritizing mental health treatment and support services is paramount to creating a criminal justice system that is fair, humane, and equitable for all, irrespective of race or background.

To achieve this goal, it is essential to invest in mental health resources both in correctional facilities and in the broader community. This includes providing access to evidence-based therapies, psychiatric care, substance abuse treatment, and psychosocial support services. Additionally, efforts should be made to address social determinants of mental health, such as poverty, unemployment, homelessness, and trauma—all of which disproportionately affect marginalized communities.

Moreover, the criminal justice system should adopt trauma-informed approaches that recognize the impact of past experiences on mental health and behavior. This entails training law enforcement officers, correctional staff, judges, and other legal professionals to recognize and respond to trauma in a sensitive and compassionate manner. It also involves implementing alternative sentencing programs, diversionary initiatives, and problem-solving courts that prioritize treatment and rehabilitation over punitive measures.

14

Furthermore, promoting community-based alternatives to incarceration, such as mental health courts, drug treatment programs, and supportive housing initiatives, can help divert individuals away from the criminal justice system and toward the support they need to address underlying mental health issues. These programs should be culturally competent, linguistically accessible, and tailored to meet the unique needs of diverse populations.

At the same time, efforts to reduce racial disparities in the criminal justice system must be prioritized, including reforming sentencing laws, eliminating discriminatory practices, and addressing systemic racism inside law enforcement agencies and court systems. This requires a commitment to equity and justice at all levels of government and society.

Ultimately, breaking the cycles of incarceration and promoting rehabilitation and healing requires a multifaceted approach that addresses the complex interplay of mental health, social, and structural factors. By prioritizing mental health treatment, investing in community-based support services, and addressing systemic inequalities, we can create a criminal justice system that upholds the dignity and rights of all, fosters healing and redemption, and promotes public safety and well-being.

Chapter 2: Our Brains

If our hearts serve as the engines propelling us forward, then our brains act as the intricate transmissions guiding our every thought and action. The human brain, a marvel of nature, stands as one of the largest and most complex organs in our bodies. At its core lies a network of cells known as neurons, serving as the building blocks of our cognitive functions.
In this analogy, neurons can be likened to legs, with axons acting as the connecting pathways. Together, neurons and axons form a complex circuitry that intricately weaves throughout the brain, potentially spanning the entire globe in its complexity.

Sigmund Freud, often hailed as the Father of Psychiatry, delved into the study of brain structure, although many of his theories leaned toward the psychological and behavioral aspects of human nature. While Freud recognized the significance of the brain in shaping human behavior, he lacked the scientific knowledge available to contemporary scientists, psychiatrists, and psychologists.

Today, we have a deeper understanding of the brain's circuitry and its influence on our thoughts and behaviors, particularly in the context of various illnesses. We have identified specific regions of the brain responsible for controlling different aspects of cognition and behavior. Notably, human beings boast the largest and most complex frontal lobes among all primates, distinguishing us in the hierarchy of cognitive evolution. Additionally, other parts of the brain, such as the parietal lobes, temporal lobes, and cerebellum, play crucial roles in regulating various functions, from sensory perception to motor coordination.

This intricate interplay of brain regions and neural pathways underscores the complexity of human cognition and behavior, offering insights into the underlying mechanisms of mental illness and neurological disorders. Through ongoing research and exploration, we continue to unravel the mysteries of the human brain, shedding light on its profound impact on our lives and the world around us.

Indeed, the brain's circuitry behaves differently in the presence of certain illnesses, further highlighting the intricacies of brain function. From schizophrenia to bipolar disorder, depression, and substance abuse, these conditions often manifest as abnormalities in neural processing, underscoring the vital role of the brain in mental health.

As our understanding of the brain continues to deepen, so too does our appreciation for its complexity and resilience. The study of brain structure and function not only advances our scientific knowledge but also holds the key to unlocking new treatments and interventions for a myriad of neurological and psychiatric conditions. In unraveling the mysteries of the brain, we pave the way for a future where mental health is understood, supported, and prioritized, ushering in a new era of well-being and understanding.

Through years of research, experiments, and studies, we have discovered that much of the control over our emotions and behavior resides within a complex network known as the limbic system. Comprising multiple structures, this system plays a pivotal role in regulating our brain's responses to stimuli and shaping our behavior.

Within the limbic system, various neurotransmitters—chemical messengers in the brain—are involved in the processing of emotions and behaviors. These neurotransmitters act much like a transmission in a car, directing and controlling the flow of signals that govern our thoughts and actions. Just as a transmission enables a car to navigate different terrains or traffic conditions, neurotransmitters modulate our brain's functions, guiding us through the complexities of daily life.

For trained and seasoned psychiatrists, understanding pharmacology—the study of these neurotransmitters and their effects—is essential. Pharmacotherapy, or the use of medications to treat mental illness, has become a cornerstone of psychiatric practice. While other therapeutic modalities, such as cognitive therapy, behavioral therapy, and psychoanalysis, are important, pharmacotherapy serves as the primary tool for directing and controlling brain function.

The majority of mental illnesses, including schizophrenia, bipolar disorder, depression, and substance abuse, stem from abnormalities in the processing of neurotransmitters within the brain. These imbalances disrupt the delicate equilibrium of brain chemistry, leading to the manifestation of symptoms characteristic of each disorder.

By targeting these neurochemical abnormalities with medications, psychiatrists can help restore balance and alleviate symptoms, enabling individuals to lead more fulfilling and productive lives. However, it is important to acknowledge that pharmacotherapy is just one component of comprehensive mental health care. Integrating various therapeutic approaches tailored to each person's needs is crucial for promoting holistic well-being and recovery.

Furthermore, our understanding of mental illness has evolved to recognize the intricate interplay between neurochemistry and behavioral manifestations. While pharmacotherapy addresses the underlying neurochemical imbalances, complementary therapeutic modalities offer additional avenues for healing and recovery.

Cognitive therapy, for instance, focuses on identifying and modifying maladaptive thought patterns and beliefs, empowering individuals to develop healthier coping mechanisms and problem-solving skills. Behavioral therapy targets observable behaviors, helping people learn new behaviors through reinforcement and conditioning techniques.

Moreover, traditional insight-oriented approaches, such as psychoanalysis, probe the unconscious mind to uncover underlying conflicts and dynamics that contribute to psychological distress. By gaining insight into these unconscious processes, people can achieve greater self-awareness and resolution of inner conflicts.

By integrating pharmacotherapy with these diverse therapeutic modalities, psychiatrists can provide comprehensive care that addresses both the biological and the psychological aspects of mental illness. This multidimensional approach not only targets symptoms but also promotes long-term resilience and well- being.

In essence, the treatment of mental illness requires a nuanced understanding of the intricate interplay among neurobiology, psychology, and environmental factors. By leveraging this holistic perspective, psychiatrists can tailor treatment plans to meet the unique needs of each patient, fostering recovery, empowerment, and hope for a brighter future.

The landscape of psychotherapy has shifted, with psychologists, social workers, licensed mental health therapists, and specialists outside the realm of psychiatry taking on the role of providing therapeutic interventions. While many of these non-psychiatrists excel in providing support and guidance, there are inherent risks in relying solely on them for addressing the core issues underlying mental illness. Such reliance is akin to changing the oil in a transmission without directly addressing the underlying mechanical issues. While this maintenance may keep the system running temporarily, it fails to address the root cause of the problem. In the realm of mental health, psychiatrists, with their specialized training in pharmacology, anatomy, and neurobiology, are uniquely positioned to examine the intricate workings of the brain and address the underlying neurochemical imbalances that contribute to mental illness.

This distinction becomes particularly crucial in underserved communities, such as Black communities, where traditional healers or religious leaders may attempt to address mental health concerns through spiritual or non-biological means. While these interventions may offer temporary relief or solace, they often fail to address the underlying neurobiological factors driving mental illness. Recognizing that the most serious psychiatric disorders stem from abnormal brain functioning underscores the importance of integrating biological and psychological perspectives in treatment.

Despite the advancements in neuroscience, psychiatrists still face challenges in diagnosing mental illness with the same precision as other medical conditions. The absence of definitive blood tests or biomarkers can sometimes lead to skepticism or misconceptions about the scientific basis of psychiatry. However, improvements in imaging techniques and neuroimaging have provided valuable insights into the neurochemical underpinnings of mental illness, shedding light on the complex interplay between brain function and behavior.

Our understanding of mental illness has evolved to recognize that many disorders, once viewed as acute or time-limited, are in fact chronic conditions requiring lifelong management. This realization underscores the importance of ongoing pharmacotherapy and other therapeutic interventions to maintain stability and improve quality of life for those living with mental illness.

While the prospect of lifelong medication may seem daunting, it is important to recognize that these medications can be life-changing for many individuals, offering relief from debilitating symptoms and enabling them to lead fulfilling lives. While there may not always be easy answers or quick fixes, the journey toward good mental health and well-being is a testament to the resilience of the human spirit and the power of scientific understanding and compassionate care.

When confronted with major mental disorders physicians are called on to embody a unique blend of tenacity, diligence, and compassion. Their training instills in them a sense of determination, not to overshadow others or elevate themselves, but rather to confront illness head-on with the knowledge that it can be managed and treated over time.

This resilience is not merely a personal attribute but a professional commitment to the well-being of their patients. It is a steadfast belief that every possible avenue of treatment must be explored and no stone left unturned in the pursuit of healing. This mindset is particularly crucial when cultural barriers or misconceptions threaten to impede the acceptance of diagnosis and treatment.

In one instance during my hospital rounds, I encountered a patient whose cultural background posed challenges to accepting a diagnosis of a treatable illness. Despite initial resistance from the patient's family, I refused to accept defeat and dove deeper into the case history. Through perseverance and collaboration with colleagues, we were able to devise a treatment plan that ultimately led to the patient's recovery and restoration to a fulfilling life.

These moments underscore the importance of cultural competence in mental health care. Understanding the norms and values of diverse communities is essential for building trust and rapport with patients and their families. In the Black community, for example, this includes understanding linguistic nuances like using the term "bad" to convey admiration or to positively highlight the importance of cultural sensitivity in communication.

How do we respond to those with major mental disorders? Physicians by nature are trained to be tenacious hard workers and overworked high achievers, and also to possess a sense of arrogance. That arrogance is not one which berates others or elevates a particular individual over another, but an arrogance of not being defeated by an illness which we know over time can be treated. We must maintain that faith and must also convey this belief to those whom we take care of. This is not to give one an unrealistic view of an illness that may require treatment but rather to pass on a belief that you will do whatever is in your power to preserve patients' lives as long as possible, and, if they have a treatable condition, that you will not give up before finding an appropriate treatment.

During one of my hospital rounds, I encountered a situation where cultural factors were impeding the acceptance of a diagnosis for one of my patients, who suffered from a treatable illness. Consulting with a colleague, I learned that the patient's cultural background posed significant barriers to acknowledging a chronic or potentially untreatable condition. As a physician, I found it impossible to accept this limitation. I could not bear the thought of informing the patient's family that we had exhausted all avenues of treatment without success.

Instead of resigning to this notion, I took a step back and sought additional information from a previous practitioner. Through diligent investigation and collaboration, we uncovered new insights that ultimately led to a successful treatment plan. Today, that young man is thriving—he has a fulfilling job and a loving family.

That experience reaffirmed my belief that refusal to accept defeat is a quality that distinguishes good physicians from great ones. It reflects the importance of persistence and advocacy in the face of adversity, ensuring that every patient receives the care and support they deserve, regardless of cultural or societal barriers.

It is imperative to ensure that therapists possess not only clinical proficiency but also a deep cultural understanding and an unflagging commitment to their patients. Cultural competence is essential in providing effective therapy, as it allows therapists to navigate and respect the unique norms and values of diverse communities.

In the Black community, for instance, linguistic nuances may shape interpretations of seemingly negative terms like "bad," which can actually connote admiration or approval. Understanding these cultural subtleties is crucial for establishing rapport and trust with patients. In the realm of therapy, cultural competence is not just a desirable trait—it is an essential aspect of effective treatment. Consider a scenario where a therapist, let's call her Dr. Smith, is working with a young Black man named Jamal who is experiencing symptoms of depression. Dr. Smith, recognizing the importance of cultural sensitivity, takes the time to understand Jamal's cultural background and how it influences his worldview and attitudes toward mental health.

During their sessions, Dr. Smith notices that Jamal often uses the term "bad" to describe positive attributes or situations, such as saying, "That party was bad!" Dr. Smith realizes that this linguistic nuance reflects a cultural norm within the Black community, where "bad" can mean good or impressive. Understanding this, Dr. Smith refrains from correcting Jamal's language and instead embraces it, recognizing it as a unique aspect of his cultural identity and focusing on the bigger picture and goal at hand.

As therapy progresses, Dr. Smith integrates Jamal's cultural beliefs and values into their treatment plan. She explores how cultural factors such as family dynamics, community support, and spiritual beliefs may impact Jamal's experience of depression. By acknowledging and validating these cultural influences, Dr. Smith creates a safe and supportive environment where Jamal feels seen, understood and respected.

However, therapy is not without its own set of unique challenges, and Jamal's family's skepticism poses a
24

significant hurdle to his mental health treatment. Despite Dr. Smith's empathetic and culturally sensitive approach, Jamal's family holds deep-seated beliefs that mental health struggles should be kept private, and seeking therapy is perceived as a sign of weakness or a deviation from cultural norms.

Recognizing the critical role of family support in Jamal's recovery, Dr. Smith approaches the situation with patience and understanding. She acknowledges the legitimacy of the family's concerns and takes proactive steps to address their misconceptions about therapy. She initiates open and respectful dialogue with Jamal's family, creating a safe space for them to express their fears and reservations and making them feel included in the process as a whole.

In these discussions, Dr. Smith provides psychoeducation about depression, its symptoms, and the various treatment options available. She emphasizes that seeking professional help is not a reflection of weakness but a proactive step toward improving Jamal's well-being. She also highlights the importance of destigmatizing mental health issues and encourages Jamal's family to prioritize his emotional health.

Additionally , Dr. Smith collaborates with Jamal's family to identify culturally relevant coping strategies and support networks that align with their values and beliefs. She respects their cultural perspectives while gently challenging harmful stereotypes and misconceptions about mental illness. Through compassionate listening and tailored guidance, Dr. Smith aims to bridge the gap between cultural traditions and modern mental health practices.

Despite initial resistance, Dr. Smith's commitment to fostering understanding and acceptance gradually leads to a shift in Jamal's family's attitudes toward therapy. They begin to recognize the value of emotional well-being and the importance of seeking professional support when needed. By actively engaging the family in the therapeutic process, Dr.

Smith strengthens their bond and creates a supportive environment conducive to Jamal's healing journey.

While navigating these challenges, Dr. Smith exemplifies the principles of culturally responsive therapy, advocating for Jamal's holistic well-being while honoring his cultural identity and familial relationships. The persistence pays off, through her dedication and perseverance, progress is made.

It is my belief that all therapists must embody resilience and perseverance, refusing to give up even in the face of challenges. This resilience extends beyond clinical techniques—it is about recognizing the inherent dignity and worth of each patient and advocating tirelessly for their well-being.

In practice, therapists encounter various obstacles that can hinder the therapeutic process. However, rather than being deterred, therapists like Dr. Smith approach these hurdles with determination and compassion.

Furthermore, therapists must also recognize the intersections of identity and mental health, understanding that individuals from diverse backgrounds may face unique challenges themselves. This requires a nuanced approach that considers cultural norms, values, and lived experiences. For example, therapists working with immigrant communities may need to consider the impact of acculturation stress or language barriers on mental health outcomes.

Additionally, therapists should be aware of how systemic issues such as racism, discrimination, and socioeconomic disparities affect mental health. For instance, minority groups often experience higher levels of stress and trauma due to exposure to racial discrimination and economic instability, which can exacerbate mental health issues.

Therapists should also consider the role of family dynamics and community support in the therapeutic process. In many cultures, family and community play a significant role in an individual's well-being, and involving them in treatment can be crucial. This might involve family therapy sessions or community-based interventions that align with the cultural practices and values of the client.

Besides, therapists need to be mindful of historical and intergenerational trauma that may affect individuals from marginalized communities. Understanding the historical context of a client's background can provide deeper insight into their current mental health struggles and help in developing more effective treatment plans.

In practice, this means actively listening to clients' stories and experiences, validating their feelings, and integrating culturally relevant strategies into therapy. It also involves continuous self-reflection and education on the part of the therapist to remain culturally competent and sensitive to the diverse needs of their clients. By adopting this holistic and inclusive approach, therapists can better support individuals from diverse backgrounds in their mental health journeys.

Chapter 3: Unraveling the Complexities of Incarceration and Mental Health Treatment

As we dive deeper into the layers of the incarcerated population, it becomes apparent that the demographic landscape is nuanced and multifaceted. While Black men constitute a significant portion of those behind bars, ranging from 30 to 40 percent - despite being only 13 percent of the population, this statistic unveils a troubling narrative of systemic injustice and social disenfranchisement. From a young age, many of these men have faced a barrage of obstacles, from inadequate educational opportunities to economic hardship, perpetuating a cycle of disadvantage that spans generations.

However, it is crucial to recognize that within this heterogeneous group, there exists a spectrum of circumstances and backgrounds. While some may indeed be classified as genuine criminals, diagnosed with antisocial personality disorder, they represent only a fraction of the incarcerated population. Among them lies an even smaller subset characterized as "super predators," described as those who are driven by a callous disregard for others and who epitomize the chilling depths of sociopathy, inflicting harm without remorse or empathy.

At a lower level of severity within the incarcerated population, we encounter individuals whose involvement with the criminal justice system arises from less egregious offenses, such as domestic disputes, substance abuse, or public disturbances. While these infractions may not pose a significant threat to public safety compared to more serious crimes, they nonetheless shed light on the complex interplay of socioeconomic factors and mental health struggles that contribute to entanglements with the law.

These offenders often find themselves caught in a web of adversity, grappling with issues such as poverty, lack of access to mental health resources, and social marginalization. For many, involvement in the criminal justice system is a manifestation of underlying struggles, rather than a deliberate choice to engage in criminal behavior. Substance abuse, for example, may be a coping mechanism for untreated mental health conditions or a response to traumatic life experiences.

Understanding the diverse backgrounds and motivations of individuals within this segment of the incarcerated population is essential for crafting effective interventions that address both their immediate needs and the systemic issues contributing to their involvement with the law. It requires a nuanced approach that acknowledges the intersectionality of factors shaping their experiences, including race, socioeconomic status, and access to resources.

Central to this approach is the recognition of people's inherent dignity and worth, regardless of their past transgressions. By prioritizing mental health treatment, substance abuse rehabilitation, and access to social support services, we can begin to address the root causes of their involvement with the criminal justice system and promote pathways to healing and recovery.

Community-reintegration efforts play a crucial role in facilitating successful transition from prison back into society. This involves providing access to stable housing, employment opportunities, and ongoing support networks to help the freed prisoners rebuild their lives and avoid reoffending.

By embracing a comprehensive approach that addresses the multifaceted needs of inmates, we can work toward breaking the cycle of incarceration and promoting holistic healing. This approach recognizes the humanity of each individual, acknowledging their potential for growth and redemption, while also addressing the broader societal inequities that perpetuate cycles of incarceration and marginalization.

Chapter 4: Unraveling the Origins: Understanding the Intersection of Mental Health Policy and Incarceration

The closure of state hospitals and the subsequent rise in the incarceration of those with mental illness can be seen as a complex interplay of historical, political, and social factors. One pivotal moment in this trajectory was the deinstitutionalization movement, catalyzed by President John F. Kennedy's Mental Health Act. While this legislation aimed to liberate individuals from the often inhumane conditions in long-term psychiatric institutions, it inadvertently led to the closure of many state hospitals without sufficient community-based support systems in place.

The deinstitutionalization era marked a shift toward community-based mental health care, emphasizing autonomy and integration. However, the reality often fell short of this ideal, as many of the mentally ill found themselves without adequate support, or access to essential services. This lack of resources and support networks left many at risk of homelessness, substance abuse, and involvement in the criminal justice system.

The implementation of tough-on-crime policies during the latter half of the twentieth century further exacerbated the situation. Instead of prioritizing mental health treatment and rehabilitation, the criminal justice system increasingly relied on punitive measures, leading to the incarceration of many with untreated mental illness. As a result, jails and prisons have become de facto warehouses for people in need of mental health care, further straining an already overburdened system.

The historical roots of psychiatric care in the United States trace back to the establishment of early asylums and hospitals, such as Friends Hospital in Pennsylvania. These institutions, initially founded with the noble intention of providing compassionate care for the mentally ill, eventually became synonymous with neglect, abuse, and institutionalization.

Dorothea Dix's advocacy for reform within the mental health care system played a pivotal role in raising awareness about the deplorable conditions in psychiatric facilities. Her tireless efforts to improve treatment and living conditions paved the way for significant reforms and laid the foundation for modern mental health care practices.

As we wrestle with the legacy of deinstitutionalization and the overrepresentation of the mentally ill in the criminal justice system, it is clear that systemic change is needed. Addressing the root causes of incarceration, such as poverty, lack of access to mental health care, and systemic inequities, requires a varied approach that prioritizes prevention, early intervention, and community-based support services.

If true reform is the goal, it is essential to advocate for policies and programs that prioritize mental health treatment, support recovery, and promote social inclusion. By addressing the structural barriers that perpetuate cycles of incarceration and marginalization, we can strive toward a more compassionate and equitable society where every individual receives the care and support they need to thrive and flourish.

The establishment of segregated psychiatric hospitals in the late nineteenth and early twentieth centuries reflected broader patterns of racial segregation and discrimination prevalent in American society. These facilities, such as the Central State Lunatic Asylum for the Colored in Virginia and the Alabama Insane Asylum, were intended to provide mental health care specifically for Black individuals. While these institutions represented a recognition of the mental health needs within Black communities, they also perpetuated racial disparities in access to care and treatment.

President Kennedy's Mental Health Act of 1963 aimed to reform mental health care by shifting away from long-term institutionalization toward community-based treatment. This approach was grounded in the belief that those with mental illness could lead fulfilling lives outside of psychiatric institutions, provided they had access to appropriate support services and resources.

However, the implementation of this vision faced significant challenges. Many psychiatric hospitals were closed, and offenders were discharged into communities that were ill-equipped to support their needs. The lack of support left many without the necessary resources to manage their conditions effectively.

As a result, numerous discharged patients struggled to navigate the complexities of the healthcare system, often facing barriers to accessing treatment and support. This, in turn, eliminates any hope of independence and sustainability for individuals who desperately want to be self-sufficient.

David Satcher, MD, PhD, made history as the first African American to lead the Centers for Disease Control and Prevention (CDC), the U.S.'s premier public health institute based in Atlanta, Georgia. The CDC's mandate is to safeguard public health by preventing and controlling diseases, injuries, and disabilities.

Dr. Satcher further distinguished himself as the first African American male to serve as Surgeon General in the United States Department of Health and Human Services (HHS) from 1998 to 2002, appointed by President Bill Clinton. A trailblazer in many respects, Dr. Satcher emphasized the importance of mental health in overall well-being, advocating for increased attention and investment in mental health conditions. In his role as the nation's chief doctor, Satcher presented a report to the president on tobacco use, focusing on the health risks of smoking for minorities and minority teenagers. He also commissioned a report on suicide prevention, sought to eliminate race-based healthcare disparities, and urged the nation to engage in an honest debate on mental health.

Throughout his career he has held top leadership positions at the Charles R. Drew University for Medicine and Science, Meharry Medical College, and the Morehouse School of Medicine where he witnessed remarkable progress in public health through medical advancements and innovative healthcare approaches. Despite these achievements, he highlighted the persistent neglect of mental health issues in national discourse. Decades later, this oversight remains apparent. Despite monumental strides in public health in recent years, mental and behavioral health concerns continue to be marginalized in our national consciousness.

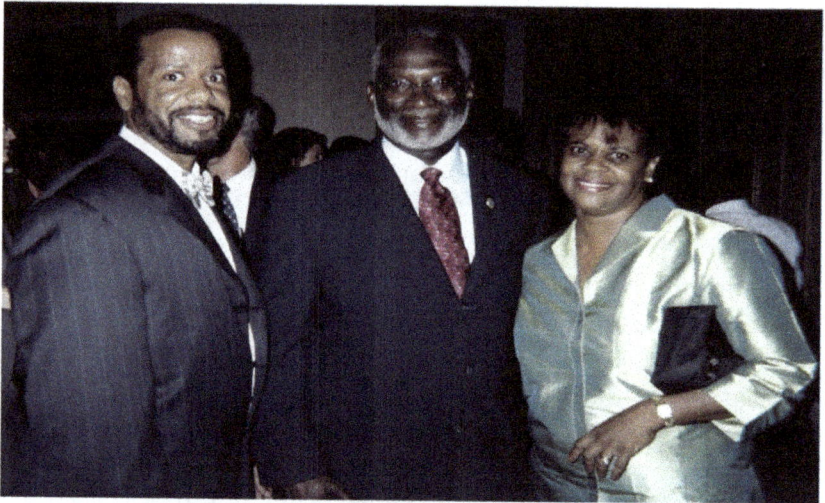

From left: Dr. Joseph Poitier, Jr.; David Satcher, MD, PhD; and Arleen Poitier

Today, the legacy of this flawed transition persists, with few notable changes. Addressing these systemic shortcomings requires a comprehensive approach that prioritizes investment in community-based mental health services, supportive housing programs, and culturally competent care. By ensuring equitable access to care and support, we can work toward breaking the cycle of incarceration and promoting healing and rehabilitation for all, regardless of race or background.

President Kennedy's concept of community-based mental health care, while visionary, faced significant challenges in implementation. Despite its noble intentions, the initiative lacked adequate funding and comprehensive planning to effectively meet the needs of the mentally ill population. Like many mental health care plans or initiatives, it suffered from a lack of support for full-circle commitment, along with the necessary financial and human capital resources required for long-term implementation and longevity.

Chronic mental illnesses requires a holistic approach to care, often referred to as "wrap-around services." This approach includes access to competent medical professionals, such as physicians and psychiatrists, who can provide appropriate treatment and medication management. Additionally, skilled social workers play a crucial role in navigating the complex health-care system and connecting patients with essential resources and support networks.

What may seem minor to some, secure housing is a fundamental cornerstone of mental health care for those with chronic illnesses. Without a safe and supportive living environment, individuals may find it difficult to maintain their mental well-being and are at an increased risk of experiencing homelessness or frequent hospitalizations. Addressing the needs of the mentally ill requires a multifaceted approach.

The challenges facing psychiatry extend beyond mere misunderstandings and misconceptions; they encompass deeply ingrained societal attitudes, systemic barriers, and the inherent complexity of mental health disorders that each present unique challenges.

The fragmentation of mental health care systems poses significant challenges. Access to mental health services varies widely depending on factors such as location, socioeconomic status, and insurance coverage. Many communities lack adequate resources, including mental health clinics, trained professionals, and affordable treatment options, exacerbating disparities in care. This lack of accessibility disproportionately affects marginalized populations, including racial and ethnic minorities, low-income individuals, and residents of rural communities. Unfortunately, those who are most in need often face the greatest barriers to accessing the care they desperately require.

Furthermore, the diagnostic process for psychiatric disorders can be complex and subjective, relying on clinical judgment and patient self-reporting. Misdiagnosis or delayed diagnosis is not uncommon, leading to ineffective treatment or inappropriate interventions. Additionally, the overlap of symptoms across different disorders can further complicate diagnosis and treatment planning.

Another challenge is the limited understanding of the underlying neurobiology of mental illness. While significant progress has been made in elucidating the biological mechanisms involved in conditions like depression, schizophrenia, and bipolar disorder, much remains unknown. The multifactorial nature of psychiatric disorders, involving genetic, environmental, and neurobiological factors, underscores the need for continued research and collaboration across disciplines.

The integration of mental health services into primary care settings remains a significant unmet need. Many receive their mental health care from primary care providers rather than specialized mental health professionals. However, primary care providers often lack adequate training in mental health assessment and management, leading to under recognition and undertreatment of psychiatric disorders.

One critical aspect is the stigma surrounding mental illness, which persists despite efforts to raise awareness and promote acceptance. Stigma can lead to discrimination, social isolation, and reluctance to seek help, perpetuating a cycle of suffering and hindering individuals from accessing the care they need. This stigma may stem from cultural beliefs, fear of the unknown, or misconceptions about mental health conditions.

The misconception and mismanagement of psychiatric care often stem from the demeanor and approach of psychiatrists themselves. Unlike other medical specialties, psychiatrists tend to be reserved, humble, and less likely to draw attention to themselves. This understated presence can lead to the perception that psychiatry is less critical or central to health care, fostering a culture where non-psychiatrists may feel emboldened to take on roles they are not fully equipped to handle.

Psychiatrists, along with neurologists and neurosurgeons, undergo rigorous training specifically tailored to disorders of the brain and of behavior. Psychiatrists, in particular, dedicate about sixteen years of their lives studying the intricacies of brain function, abnormal behavior resulting from neurochemical imbalances, and effective treatment modalities for various brain disorders. While neurologists focus on conditions affecting movement and brain structure, and neurosurgeons specialize in surgical interventions when necessary, psychiatrists possess a unique expertise in managing the complex interplay between the brain and behavior.

However, the roles of social workers, psychologists, and mental health therapists should not be discounted. While their expertise lies in different domains, they play valuable roles in providing support and therapy to individuals with mental health challenges. Yet their scope of practice differs significantly from that of medical professionals trained to manage brain disorders comprehensively.

Unfortunately, within the Black community and beyond, there is often a reliance on these alternative disciplines, leading to a dilution of psychiatric care. This reliance may stem from a lack of access to psychiatrists or misconceptions about the role of psychiatry in mental health care. In reality, Black psychiatrists represent only a small fraction of mental health professionals nationwide, further exacerbating disparities in access to quality psychiatric care. For every hundred psychiatrists, only one may be Black.

To address these challenges, efforts must be made to increase awareness about the unique contributions of psychiatrists and to expand access to psychiatric services, particularly in underserved communities. This includes advocating for increased funding for psychiatric training programs, incentivizing psychiatrists to practice in underserved areas, and implementing community outreach programs to raise awareness about mental health issues and available resources. By promoting a greater understanding of the critical role psychiatrists play in mental health care, we can work toward ensuring that individuals receive the comprehensive and specialized care they need to achieve optimal mental well-being.

Addressing the systemic racism embedded within the health care and criminal justice systems is crucial for understanding and dismantling the barriers to mental health care access faced by Blacks. Historically, Black communities have endured centuries of systemic oppression and discrimination, resulting in disparities across various social determinants of health, including access to health care. Structural racism manifests in unequal access to quality health-care facilities, limited health insurance coverage, and implicit biases among health-care providers, all of which contribute to disparities in mental-health-care access and outcomes.

In the criminal justice system, racial bias and discrimination are pervasive, leading to disproportionately high rates of

40

incarceration among Black people. The historical mistreatment of Black people by the health-care system, such as in the Tuskegee Syphilis Study and forced sterilization campaigns, has fostered mistrust and skepticism toward medical institutions. This legacy of medical exploitation has contributed to reluctance among some in the Black community to seek mental health care, further perpetuating disparities in access and utilization.

To address these entrenched disparities, it is imperative to confront them head-on. This includes implementing anti-racist policies and practices, enhancing diversity and cultural competence among healthcare providers, building trust, increasing transparency and investing in community-based mental health resources specifically tailored to meet the needs of the Black population.

Additionally, advocating for policy reforms that prioritize mental health parity, expand access to affordable health care, and promote alternatives to incarceration for individuals with mental illness are essential steps toward achieving equity in mental-health-care access and outcomes.

Ultimately, achieving mental health equity requires a comprehensive approach that addresses the intersecting social, economic, and racial determinants of health while centering the voices and experiences of those most impacted by systemic inequities. Black people are disproportionately impacted by policies and practices that perpetuate mass incarceration and punitive approaches to addressing social issues. Racial profiling, discriminatory sentencing practices, and over-policing of Black communities contribute to higher rates of arrest and incarceration of members of those communities, many of whom struggle with untreated mental health conditions.

Once intertwined in the criminal justice system, Black people face additional barriers to accessing mental health care.

Correctional facilities often lack adequate mental health resources, leading to unmet treatment needs and aggravation of mental health symptoms. Moreover, stigma surrounding mental illness can deter inmates from seeking help and lead to inadequate or inappropriate treatment.

Additionally, direct efforts to address systemic racism must be prioritized. This requires ongoing education, training, and accountability to challenge implicit biases and discriminatory practices. In addition to training law enforcement officers and correctional staff in crisis intervention and de-escalation techniques, there is a pressing need for increased mental health literacy among these professionals. This involves educating them about the signs and symptoms of mental illness, as well as strategies for effectively communicating with those experiencing psychiatric crises. By enhancing their understanding of mental health issues, officers and staff can better identify when someone may need mental health support and respond in a manner that prioritizes their safety and well-being.

Furthermore, community-based mental health services must be expanded and strengthened to ensure access to timely and appropriate care. This involves increasing funding for mental health clinics, crisis hotlines, and mobile crisis teams capable of providing on-the-ground support to individuals in need. Additionally, efforts should be made to integrate mental health services into primary care settings and other community-based organizations to ensure support is available in familiar and accessible environments, thereby promoting engagement and participation.

Diversion programs play a crucial role in redirecting individuals with mental illness away from the criminal justice system and toward appropriate treatment and support. These programs, such as mental health courts, pretrial diversion programs, and crisis intervention teams, offer alternatives to incarceration for individuals whose offenses stem from their mental health condition. By connecting these individuals to community-based treatment and support services, diversion programs can help break the cycle of incarceration and facilitate recovery and rehabilitation through alternative care.

Collaboration and communication among mental health providers, law enforcement agencies, and the criminal justice system are essential for ensuring that mentally ill persons receive the support and treatment they need. This includes establishing protocols for information sharing and coordination of care, as well as developing joint training programs to enhance collaboration among different stakeholders. By working together, these entities can ensure that individuals with mental illness are provided with comprehensive and unified coordinated support throughout their involvement with the criminal justice system.

Expanding mental health literacy and awareness within Black communities involves implementing community-based initiatives that educate people about mental health disorders, symptoms, and available treatment options. These initiatives can include workshops, seminars, and support groups held in accessible locations such as community centers, churches, and schools. By providing accurate information and resources, these programs empower people to recognize when they or their loved ones may be experiencing mental health challenges and to seek help without fear of stigma or discrimination. Culturally tailored outreach programs play a crucial role in engaging Black communities and addressing cultural norms and beliefs related to mental health.

Efforts to address systematic barriers to access to mental health care require advocacy and policy change at both the local and national levels. This includes advocating for increased funding for mental health services in underserved communities, expanding Medicaid and other insurance coverage to include comprehensive mental health care, and implementing workforce diversity initiatives to increase the representation of Black mental health professionals.

Promoting mental health resilience and well-being within Black communities involves empowering people to prioritize self-care practices and build supportive networks of care. This can include providing education and resources on stress management, coping skills, and healthy lifestyle habits. Additionally, fostering community connections and social support networks can help people feel more connected and supported, reducing feelings of isolation and improving overall mental well-being.

Chapter 5: Navigating Health Care for Incarcerated Individuals and Marginalized Communities

Providing health care to incarcerated individuals and marginalized communities poses unique challenges that demand careful consideration and sensitivity from health-care providers. In this chapter, we explore the complexities of navigating health-care delivery in these contexts, addressing issues of cultural competence, power dynamics, and access to care. We examine the importance of fostering trust, empathy, and inclusivity in health-care interactions, and we propose strategies for promoting health equity and improving outcomes for all, regardless of their circumstances.

The relationship between doctor and patient is often regarded as a cornerstone of effective health-care delivery. Ideally, these interactions are characterized by genuineness, empathy, and mutual respect, fostering an environment where patients feel valued and supported. However, in reality, achieving this level of rapport can be challenging, particularly when considering the diverse cultural backgrounds and lived experiences of patients.

Cultural sensitivity plays a crucial role in shaping the doctor–patient relationship, as health-care providers must navigate the nuances and intricacies of each patient's cultural background. While it is not necessarily essential for a patient to be cared for by a health-care provider of the same race or ethnicity, it is imperative that the caretaker demonstrate an understanding of the patient's cultural norms, values, and communication styles. This awareness enables health-care providers to tailor their approach to meet the unique needs and preferences of each individual, fostering trust and rapport in the process.

The question of whether mental health patients do better when treated by professionals of their own race or ethnicity is complex and nuanced, and research findings have varied. Cultural competence refers to a therapist's ability to understand and respect the cultural backgrounds, beliefs, and values of their clients. Therapists who are culturally competent may be better equipped to establish rapport, understand the unique stressors and experiences of their clients, and tailor treatment approaches accordingly. This can potentially lead to better outcomes for minority clients.

Some clients may feel more comfortable and understood when working with therapists who share their racial or ethnic background. This comfort and sense of connection can positively impact the therapeutic relationship and engagement in treatment.

Diversity among mental health professionals can contribute to a more comprehensive understanding of mental health issues and better responsiveness to the diverse needs of clients. This includes not only racial and ethnic diversity but also diversity in perspectives, experiences, and approaches to treatment.

Ultimately, the effectiveness of therapy depends significantly on the therapist's skills, training, and ability to apply evidence-based practices. Competent therapists from any racial or ethnic background can effectively treat clients of diverse backgrounds when they are trained in culturally sensitive approaches.

In some cases, minority clients may face barriers to accessing mental health care, including a lack of providers from similar racial or ethnic backgrounds. Increasing the diversity of the mental health workforce can help improve access to care and address disparities in mental health outcomes. However, even when providers from similar racial or ethnic backgrounds are available, there is no guarantee that those seeking treatment will be able to be seen or accepted as new patients within a reasonable amount of time. Many of these practitioners are in high demand and have limited or no availability to accept new patients, prioritizing the quality of care for existing patients under their care.

Research findings on the impact of therapist-client racial or ethnic match on outcomes have been mixed. Some studies suggest modest benefits for match, particularly in terms of client satisfaction and perceived cultural understanding, while others find no significant difference in clinical outcomes based on therapist-client racial or ethnic match.

Overall, while cultural competence and client preferences for racial or ethnic match can play a role in mental health treatment outcomes, what matters most is the therapist's ability to provide effective, evidence-based care in a culturally sensitive manner. Training therapists in cultural competence and increasing diversity within the mental health workforce are important steps toward improving outcomes and addressing disparities in mental health care.

In the context of Black communities, cultural competence is particularly crucial, as certain expressions and phrases may carry different meanings than in other cultural contexts. As discussed in Chapter Two, the term "bad" may be used colloquially within the Black population to express admiration or approval, whereas it might be understood differently by individuals from different backgrounds. By understanding and respecting these cultural nuances, health care providers can ensure that their interactions with patients are respectful, inclusive, and conducive to effective communication and care. This cultural sensitivity fosters trust and enhances the therapeutic relationship, ultimately improving health outcomes for Black patients.

In colloquial language within Black communities, the term "bad" is often used as a compliment rather than a criticism. When someone is described as a "bad chick" or a "bad brother," it is not meant to imply that they look unattractive or poorly dressed. Instead, it is a way of expressing admiration for their appearance, style, or demeanor.

This usage of the word "bad" highlights the nuanced nature of language and how meanings can vary within different cultural contexts. In this case, "bad" has been reappropriated to convey positive qualities, adding richness and depth to expressions of admiration and appreciation in Black communities.

In many Black communities, there is a common misconception regarding diabetes, often referred to simply as "sugar" or "sugar diabetes." This misconception stems from the belief that consuming sugar directly causes diabetes, which is unfortunately prevalent but inaccurate. While it is true that elevated glucose levels are a characteristic feature of diabetes, the condition itself is much more complex and multifaceted. Diabetes is a chronic metabolic disorder characterized by the body's inability to properly regulate blood sugar levels, leading to persistently high blood glucose levels.

Several factors contribute to diabetes, including genetic predisposition, lifestyle factors such as diet and exercise, and underlying health conditions. Consuming excessive amounts of sugar can certainly contribute to the risk of developing type 2 diabetes, particularly when combined with other risk factors such as obesity and sedentary behavior. However, sugar consumption alone does not directly cause diabetes.

Thus, it is important to educate the Black community about the role of genetics, lifestyle factors, and overall health in the development and management of diabetes. By increasing awareness and understanding of diabetes, we can empower Black people to make informed choices about their health and reduce the prevalence of this chronic condition.

The resistance of Black people to receiving medical care, particularly from White doctors, is deeply entrenched in

48

historical and cultural contexts. For generations, African diaspora communities have cultivated their own healing traditions, which often incorporate herbal remedies, spiritual rituals, and communal support systems. These practices reflect a holistic understanding of health that emphasizes the interconnectedness of the body, mind, and spirit.

Moreover, the history of medical exploitation and mistreatment of Black people has fostered a profound distrust of the health- care system. As mentioned before, from the era when slaves were subjected to medical experimentation without consent, to the twentieth century atrocities such as the Tuskegee syphilis study—in which Black men were deliberately denied treatment for syphilis—these egregious acts have left deep scars on the collective psyche of Black communities. The enduring legacy of these injustices continues to shape perceptions of health care among the Black population, leading to skepticism and reluctance to engage with medical institutions.

In the field of psychiatry, the mistreatment of patients has been particularly egregious. Historical treatment methods, including forced institutionalization, electroconvulsive therapy without sedation, lobotomies, insulin comas, and iced baths, reflect a disturbing disregard for the dignity and well-being of those with mental illness. These practices not only failed to provide effective treatment but also perpetuated trauma and suffering.

Given this history of exploitation and abuse, it is understandable that many Black people harbor skepticism toward psychiatric professionals, especially those who are not from their own community. Building trust and addressing the unique needs of Black patients requires a careful approach that acknowledges and respects the historical and cultural factors shaping their healthcare experiences. This includes ensuring representation of Black professionals in mental health fields, providing culturally responsive care, and actively working to

49

change the narrative regarding equity in mental health care. These efforts are essential to creating a healthcare environment where Black patients feel understood, respected, and supported in their mental health journeys.

The health-care disparities in jails and prisons are indeed pervasive and profoundly impactful, particularly for marginalized Black and Brown communities. These disparities are varied, stemming from a combination of structural inequities and longstanding disparities in access to health care.

One significant factor contributing to health-care disparities in correctional facilities is the lack of adequate resources and infrastructure to address the complex medical and mental health needs of inmates. Many jails and prisons are overcrowded, understaffed, and under-resourced, leading to substandard conditions and limited access to medical care. This often results in delayed or denied treatment for chronic conditions, mental illness, and other health-care needs, exacerbating health disparities.

Moreover, there is a lack of continuity of care for offenders transitioning from incarceration back into the community. Many inmates leave correctional facilities without access to essential medications, follow-up appointments, or support services, increasing their risk of relapse, deterioration of health, and reincarceration. This disruption in care perpetuates a cycle of poor health outcomes and recidivism, further entrenching health-care disparities among former prisoners.

Additionally, racial disparities in the criminal justice system contribute to disproportionate rates of incarceration among Black and Brown people, who are more likely to experience harsher sentencing, racial profiling, and systemic discrimination. As a result, these communities bear the brunt of health-care disparities, facing greater barriers to accessing timely and appropriate medical and mental health care.

Addressing healthcare disparities in jails and prisons demands a well-planned and meticulously executed approach that tackles both systemic issues and the broader social determinants of health affecting incarcerated populations. This involves implementing policies to enhance healthcare access and quality, expanding diversion programs and alternatives to incarceration, and advocating for comprehensive reforms to combat systemic racism and inequality. Shifting the narrative and broadening the scope of discussions are crucial steps toward achieving improved health outcomes and successful reintegration into society for individuals affected by incarceration.

In the United States, approximately ten million people struggle with serious mental illnesses like schizophrenia, depression, or bipolar disorder. Within the Black population, the prevalence of serious mental illness stands at 20 percent, despite making up roughly 13 percent of the total population. Despite these statistics, Black and Brown communities are disproportionately represented in the criminal justice system, making up nearly 30 to 40 percent of the jail population.

Beyond incarceration, Black people encounter stigma surrounding mental illness, both within their communities and in broader society. This stigma can hinder access to appropriate care and support. Compounding the issue, Black patients are more likely to rely on psychiatric emergency services than on community-based support services, and they experience higher rates of involuntary hospitalization.

Furthermore, interactions with law enforcement often result in emergency mental health treatment for Black people at disproportionately high rates. This overrepresentation extends to clinical settings, where Black patients are more frequently diagnosed with schizophrenia and prescribed higher doses of antipsychotic medication compared to their White counterparts. Paradoxically, despite facing greater mental health challenges, Black patients are less likely to receive interventions for co- occurring disorders such as depression and substance abuse.

People in jails and prisons face significantly higher rates of mental health challenges compared to the general population. For instance, they are twenty-five times more likely to experience psychotic disorders and three times more likely to commit suicide. The experience of being incarcerated intensifies these issues, subjecting them to immediate stressors upon entry.

Upon being booked into a jail or prison, inmates are stripped of their privacy and identity, thrust into an environment where intimidation, harassment, and even physical violence are commonplace. This can come both from fellow inmates and occasionally from corrections officers, who may be dealing with their own challenges.

Further, the structured environment of incarceration disrupts normal circadian rhythms, as inmates may be confined to cells without access to sunlight or clocks to mark the passage of time. The quality and quantity of food provided are often subpar, with inmates sometimes having to navigate power dynamics to secure adequate nourishment.

Most troublingly, the loss of dignity is pervasive within correctional facilities, and for Black inmates this loss is often magnified by systemic racism and biases. These challenges demonstrate the urgent need for reforms to prioritize mental health support, ensure humane treatment of inmates, and address racial disparities that perpetuate injustice.

No one wants to be relegated to the lowest rung of the care system or the socioeconomic ladder. This sentiment has deep historical roots, dating back to the era of slavery in the United States. During that dark period of history, many Black people sought refuge from the brutalities of the South by fleeing to the North, where they hoped to find greater dignity and

52

opportunities for advancement. Regrettably, echoes of these disparities persist to this day.

An illuminating anecdote from my time working in the acute-care area of the jail illustrates this point poignantly. During one of my routine assessments for acute suicide risk, I encountered an inmate who made a striking assertion: "I am not Black." He went on to explain that he should not be subjected to the mistreatment experienced by other inmates, particularly those with darker skin tones whom he identified as Black. This declaration revealed a stark reality: within the confines of the criminal justice system, race continues to shape prisoners' experiences and treatment, even among those who may seek to distance themselves from their racial identity. My encounter serves as a sobering reminder of the enduring impact of systemic racism and inequality in the criminal justice system.

The revelation that this individual, who perceived himself as not Black despite his darker complexion, left me both amazed and astounded. As a Black man myself, it struck me that he was two shades darker than I am, yet he vehemently disassociated himself from the label of Blackness.

His assertion carried profound implications, reflecting a deep-seated desire to distance himself from the historical traumas and injustices inflicted on Black slaves. In his mind, identifying as Black meant aligning himself with a legacy of torment, degradation, and violence—a legacy that he sought to escape or deny.

What he was conveying to me went beyond a simple assertion of his racial identity; it was a plea for recognition of his humanity and a demand for respect that transcended the color of his skin. This sentiment, though startling, resonates with broader societal attitudes toward race and identity. Even today, many individuals may downplay or disavow their black or brown skin color, seeking to evade the societal burdens and stereotypes associated with racial identity. It shows the enduring impact of historical trauma and systemic racism on individual perceptions of self and identity, highlighting the complex and multifaceted nature of racial identity in contemporary society.

This phenomenon is not confined to the walls of a jail cell; it is pervasive in communities across the country, including here in Miami. Immigrants of African descent, whose ancestors may have arrived on the same slave ships as African Americans, often reject the label of Black American in favor of preserving their own cultural identity and distancing themselves from the stigma of slavery.

At its core, this is a plea for dignity and respect—a fundamental human desire shared by those of all backgrounds. Nobody wants to be associated with a group that has been systematically dehumanized and oppressed. While that is a sobering reality, it is also a sign of the enduring legacy of slavery and the ongoing struggle for racial equality and justice.

This discord among people of African descent, particularly those who have immigrated from the Caribbean islands and countries of Africa, stems from a complex interplay of historical, cultural, and sociopolitical factors. It underscores the importance of understanding and preserving one's history, even when it is painful or inconvenient.

The desire to distance oneself from the legacy of slavery and racial oppression is understandable, given the deep scars it has left on the collective psyche of Black communities worldwide. This history, often hidden or downplayed, shapes the way individuals perceive themselves and their place in society.

The fear of assimilation and the "browning" of America reflects broader anxieties about demographic shifts and changing power dynamics. Non-Black individuals may feel threatened by these changes, leading to resistance and discrimination against Black communities.

For people of African descent, navigating these complexities requires a reevaluation of their relationships with African Americans and a recognition of the shared struggles and experiences that bind them together. The legacy of slavery and racism has affected Black people around the world, regardless of their geographic origin.

It is natural for individuals to seek survival and respect in a society that often denies them both based on their race. The young man's reluctance to identify as Black American underscores the universal human desire for dignity and acceptance, even in the face of systemic injustice.

Ultimately, confronting these discordant narratives and forging solidarity among people of African descent is essential for building a more inclusive and equitable society. It requires acknowledging the painful truths of the past while working toward a future where all individuals, regardless of race or background, are treated with dignity and respect.

As Black people, we have internalized the narrative of inferiority propagated by the institution of slavery and its aftermath. We have been conditioned to believe that our worth is inherently less than that of our White counterparts, perpetuating feelings of inadequacy and self-doubt.

Despite the progress made in the fight for civil rights, the struggle for equality and justice persists. In 2024 we still find ourselves advocating not just for civil rights, but for fundamental human rights for minorities and those with darker skin tones. The color of our skin should not determine our access to opportunity, justice, or dignity.

It is disheartening to realize that in the twenty-first century, we are still suffering the same injustices and disparities that have plagued our communities for generations. The fact that melanin levels dictate the treatment and opportunities afforded to human beings is a stark reminder of the entrenched racism and inequality that permeate our society.

The disparities we see today—whether in education, health care, employment, or the criminal justice system—are rooted in this legacy of slavery and systemic racism. Until we address the underlying structures that perpetuate inequality and dismantle systems of oppression, true equality will remain elusive. It is incumbent on us to continue the fight for justice and equality, striving to create a world where every individual, regardless of race, can thrive and flourish without fear of discrimination or prejudice.

Doing no harm encompasses not only avoiding direct physical harm but also ensuring that interventions, treatments, and decisions are made with the utmost consideration for their potential risks and benefits. It requires careful deliberation and ethical reflection to ensure that the actions uphold the highest standards of patient care and respect for autonomy.

When medical professionals deviate from this principle, whether through actions that result in physical harm, emotional distress, or a breach of trust, they undermine the foundation of the patient–provider relationship and jeopardize the integrity of medical practice as a whole. In the pursuit of healing and alleviating suffering, it is imperative that health-care providers remain vigilant in upholding the principle of primum non nocere, serving as steadfast advocates for the well-being and dignity of those under their care. Primum non nocere is a Latin phrase that means "first, do no harm". The phrase is sometimes recorded as primum nil nocere and often associated with the original Hippocratic Oath. Although the phrase does not appear in the AD 245 version of the oath, similar intentions are vowed by, "I will abstain from all intentional wrong-doing and harm".

Chapter 6: Upholding the Oath: Primum Non Nocere in African American Health Care

As Black physicians, we carry the weight of history and the collective experiences of our community when it comes to health care. We understand that trust is not easily given, especially in a system that has often failed our community in the past. Therefore, we approach every patient interaction with a deep sense of responsibility and commitment to ensuring informed consent.

In the case of the elderly lady I encountered in the emergency room, I recognized the importance of transparent communication and empowerment. I took the time to explain to her, in clear and understandable terms, the reasons behind her hospitalization and the proposed course of treatment. I made sure to address any concerns or questions she had, allowing her to actively participate in decisions about her care.

Drawing on my expertise in psychiatry and forensic psychiatry, I was able to navigate the complexities of the situation with sensitivity and empathy. I understood the intersection of medical treatment and legal implications, ensuring that the patient's autonomy and rights were respected at every step.

For Black physicians, obtaining informed consent is not just a procedural requirement—it is a profound acknowledgment of the dignity and agency of our patients. It is a reaffirmation of our commitment to upholding ethical standards and advocating for the well-being of those we serve, even in the face of historical injustices and systemic challenges.

A few days later, I found myself pondering a troubling realization: my competence had been doubted by another attending physician at the hospital, who happened to be White and seemed intent on using me as a target for ridicule. This incident unfolded prominently during a "morbidity and mortality" conference, a platform typically convened when there is uncertainty about a patient's diagnosis or when an adverse event occurs. What struck me deeply was the demographic makeup of the attendees—all predominately White colleagues—from whom I had previously earned respect but who now seemed to view me through a different lens. This observation raised profound questions about diversity and inclusivity in medical environments.

Adding to my discomfort was the unexpected presence of an attorney from the Public Defender's Office, a role typically involved in advocating for the mentally ill during involuntary hospitalization petitions. As the sole double-board-certified psychiatrist in the room, drawing from fifteen years of experience in a correctional facility, I could not help but feel a mix of frustration and concern regarding the apparent disregard or devaluation of my expertise in such contexts.

I have always kept in mind the Tuskegee experiment. The Tuskegee Syphilis Study, conducted by the U.S. Public Health Service (USPHS) from 1932 to 1972 in Alabama, involved 600 Black men—399 with latent syphilis and 201 without the disease. The study aimed to observe the natural progression of untreated syphilis under the guise of offering free healthcare. Participants were misled to believe they were receiving treatment for "bad blood," a term used to describe various ailments.

Even after penicillin became the standard treatment for syphilis in 1947, participants were not provided with the antibiotic. Instead, they received placebos and ineffective treatments. Crucially, participants were not informed of their true diagnosis or the study's real purpose, exploiting their socioeconomic vulnerabilities. As a result, many suffered severe health issues, died from syphilis-related complications, and the disease was transmitted to family members.

58

The study was exposed in 1972 by a whistleblower, leading to its termination and widespread public outrage. This scandal prompted significant changes in research ethics, including the establishment of the National Research Act in 1974, the Belmont Report in 1979, and the implementation of Institutional Review Boards (IRBs) to ensure ethical standards in research involving human subjects.

The Tuskegee Syphilis Study significantly eroded trust in the healthcare system among African American communities, contributing to ongoing health disparities. In 1997, President Bill Clinton formally apologized on behalf of the U.S. government, and compensation and health benefits were provided to the study's survivors and their families. The Tuskegee Syphilis Study remains a pivotal example of unethical medical research, underscoring the necessity for rigorous ethical standards to protect vulnerable populations.

I wanted to blurt out in that room, "Do you think that I, as a Black person, would subject anybody to what happened to my people such as those men who risked their lives, not only in war, but in the health- care field to help us learn about disease, men who were fooled and lied to. Do you actually think I would do this to a person?"

The experience of having my expertise questioned in a professional setting was deeply frustrating and disheartening. With my credentials and extensive experience in a challenging environment like the jail system, I felt a sense of disbelief that my qualifications and judgment were being called into question.

The morbidity and mortality conference, typically a forum for learning and reflection, turned into a moment of indignation and frustration for me. To add to my dismay, all the attendees were predominately White, intensifying the sense of isolation and misunderstanding I felt in that moment.

Reflecting on the Tuskegee experiment, where Black men were subjected to unethical medical treatment without their consent, I was acutely aware of the historical context that shaped my perception of the situation. The memory of those men, who were deceived and mistreated in the name of medical research, resonated deeply with me.

In that room, I grappled with the urge to confront the implicit biases and assumptions that seemed to underpin the questioning of my expertise. I wanted to assert my identity as a Black physician, to challenge the notion that I would ever perpetuate harm or unethical practices against my patients. However, I also recognized the importance of professionalism and restraint in such situations. Despite my anger and frustration, I chose not to confront the person that orchestrated this fiasco. Instead, I resolved to continue advocating for the principles of ethical practice and cultural competency in my work, striving to challenge stereotypes and biases through my actions and leadership.

Despite the attempt at ridicule, most of the young residents in training enjoyed working with me and learned a lot from me. I was presented with an embroidered University of Miami jersey upon leaving the hospital as a going away gift. I am sure these residents have no idea just how much that shirt meant to me as a token of their appreciation and acknowledgement as someone who made a difference in their lives.

The experiences of abuse, disrespect, and systemic discrimination that Black people have endured throughout history have left a deep imprint on our collective consciousness. These injustices, rooted in racism and white supremacy, have shaped our understanding of autonomy and consent, particularly in the context of health care.

As a Black physician, I am acutely aware of the importance of giving patients full agency over their own bodies and health-care decisions. Our history of being marginalized and denied basic rights underscores the significance of respecting individual autonomy and ensuring informed consent at every step of the medical process.

Therefore, it was disheartening and frustrating to be accused of not affording someone the opportunity to make decisions about their own health care. Such accusations not only undermined my integrity as a physician but also disregarded the foundational principles of patient-centered care and respect for autonomy.

In my practice, I am committed to upholding the values of transparency, empathy, and respect for every individual, regardless of their race or background. I strive to create a safe and empowering environment where patients feel heard, valued, and fully informed about their health-care options.

Moving forward, I remain steadfast in my dedication to advocating for the rights and dignity of all patients, particularly those from marginalized communities who have historically been disenfranchised and disempowered. It is through upholding these principles that we can work toward a more just and equitable health-care system for everyone.

As a Black man, the specter of the syphilis study looms large in my consciousness. Its shadow extends beyond the pages of history, casting a long and somber reminder of the systemic exploitation and betrayal endured by our community. Witnessing the repercussions of medical malfeasance firsthand, particularly in the form of young Black men contorted in agony from the adverse effects of potent medications, serves as a visceral reminder of the enduring disparities and injustices embedded in our health-care system.

In my role as a health-care provider, I have confronted the stark reality of these injustices, wrestling with the harsh truth that individuals, especially those from marginalized communities, continue to be denied their fundamental rights and access to adequate medical care. The glaring inequalities in our legal and criminal justice systems further compound these injustices, perpetuating cycles of dehumanization and oppression.

I come from a background where I prioritized dignity, respect, and individual autonomy for every person under my care. When assessing the treatment options for an elderly lady, my foremost concern was to ensure that she felt empowered and informed about her health-care decisions. That was not a situation necessitating complex surgical procedures or life-altering interventions; rather, it was about providing medication to alleviate her symptoms and improve her well-being.

Despite my dedication to upholding the principles of informed consent and patient autonomy, I found myself scrutinized by a colleague who questioned my judgment. It is hard not to see this as a reflection of the systemic biases and prejudices that continue to pervade our society, particularly in professional settings. As a Black health-care provider, I am acutely aware of the insidious ways in which racial biases can influence perceptions of competence and authority.

What my colleague failed to recognize was my expertise and certification in navigating the delicate intersection of mental health treatment and legal considerations. I have undergone rigorous training to ensure that the rights and autonomy of individuals with mental illness are upheld and respected. In contrast, my colleague lacked this specialized knowledge and perspective. Thus, that raises the question: Who is better equipped to safeguard the rights and dignity of those under our care?

Sitting in that room, surrounded by colleagues whose privilege shielded them from the harsh realities faced by marginalized communities, I could not help but feel a sense of indignation.

Here I was, a Black physician with years of experience navigating the complexities of mental health care, being questioned and undermined simply because of the color of my skin.

It was a stark reminder of the insidious nature of racism in the health-care system, where biases often lurk beneath the surface, shaping interactions and decisions in subtle yet profound ways. Despite my expertise and qualifications, I was made to feel like an outsider, my perspective dismissed and my authority undermined
.
But beyond the personal affront, this incident underscored a broader truth about the unequal power dynamics that exist in the doctor–patient relationship. For far too long, marginalized communities, particularly Black communities, have been subjected to paternalistic and sometimes harmful treatment at the hands of health-care providers who fail to see them as equals.

As a Black physician, I carry with me the weight of history—a history marked by exploitation, discrimination, and disregard for Black lives. Even in the face of such adversity, I remain steadfast in my commitment to upholding the principles of ethical health care and advocating for the rights and dignity of every patient. It is a constant battle, fraught with challenges and obstacles, but one that I am determined to fight with every fiber of my being.

In the end, the true measure of a health-care system lies not in its technological advancements or medical breakthroughs, but in its ability to treat every patient with compassion, respect, and dignity—regardless of their race, ethnicity, or socioeconomic status. And until we achieve true equity and justice in health care, my work will never be done.

Chapter 7: Healing the Breach: Navigating the Doctor–Patient Relationship in Black Health Care

In the intricate dance of health care, the relationship between doctor and patient is paramount. It is a sacred bond built on trust, empathy, and mutual respect—a bond that transcends mere diagnosis and treatment, implicating the very essence of human connection. Yet for Black individuals navigating the labyrinth of the health-care system, this relationship is often fraught with complexities, shaped by historical injustices, systemic biases, and cultural nuances.

In this chapter, we delve deep into the dynamics of the doctor–patient relationship, exploring the unique challenges faced by Black patients and physicians alike. From the legacy of medical exploitation to the pervasive impact of racism in health care, we confront uncomfortable truths and seek pathways to healing and reconciliation.

As we peel back the layers of this complex relationship, we uncover stories of resilience, empowerment, and advocacy. Through the lens of personal experiences and professional insights, we strive to bridge the gap between theory and practice, illuminating the pathways to a more equitable and compassionate health-care system for all. Join us on this journey as we navigate the twists and turns of the doctor–patient relationship, seeking to heal the breach and forge a brighter future for Black health care.

The doctor–patient relationship is often characterized by a fiduciary bond, rooted in the mutual understanding that patients entrust their health and well-being to their physicians. Patients pay for medical services, and in return, physicians are entrusted with the responsibility to provide the highest standard of care with integrity and expertise.

However, it is important to recognize that physicians are also human beings with personal and financial obligations. While many enter the medical profession out of a desire to serve and heal, they must also navigate the practicalities of daily life. This includes providing for their families, managing bills, and striving for a semblance of work–life balance amid demanding schedules.

Medical professionals often sacrifice personal time and familial obligations in service to their patients. They may work long hours, be on call at all hours of the day and night, and miss important milestones in their loved ones' lives. This sacrifice is inherent in the calling of medicine, but it underscores the dedication and commitment that physicians bring to their profession despite their personal sacrifices.

The doctor–patient relationship is often described as fiduciary, meaning that physicians are entrusted with the well-being of their patients and are expected to act in their best interests. This trust is foundational to the practice of medicine, as patients rely on their doctors to provide expert guidance, compassionate care, and effective treatment.

For many health-care providers, medicine is not merely a job but a calling—a vocation driven by a deep sense of duty and commitment to healing. Despite these challenges, the satisfaction derived from helping others and making a positive impact on patients' lives is a powerful motivator.

While most physicians approach their work with integrity and professionalism, there are inevitably instances of misconduct or negligence. However, these outliers should not overshadow the dedication and compassion exhibited by the vast majority.

It has been observed that many good doctors prioritize patient care over financial gain, sometimes to their own financial detriment. This is not to say that financial stability is unimportant, but rather that the primary focus remains on delivering high-quality care and achieving positive outcomes for patients.

Patients entrust their health and well-being to their physicians, who in turn strive to uphold the highest standards of medical ethics and professionalism in their practice.

The perception of physicians as arrogant, condescending, or disrespectful to their patients is a stereotype that unfortunately persists in some quarters. While there may be instances when individual doctors exhibit such behavior, it is essential to recognize that these traits are not representative of the medical profession as a whole.

In reality, the vast majority of physicians are deeply committed to providing compassionate, patient-centered care. They undergo rigorous training and adhere to professional standards aimed at fostering positive doctor–patient relationships built on trust, empathy, and respect.

However, like any profession, medicine is not immune to power dynamics or interpersonal conflicts. In hierarchical health-care environments, such as hospitals or academic institutions, there may be times when individuals in positions of authority misuse their power to assert dominance or control over physicians.

This dynamic can manifest in various ways, such as belittling or undermining doctors' expertise, micromanaging their clinical decisions, or dismissing their concerns and input. Such behavior not only erodes trust and collaboration but also undermines the quality of patient care.

Addressing these issues requires a commitment to fostering a culture of respect, professionalism, and collaboration. Leaders must actively promote mutual respect among all members of the health-care team and create channels for open communication and constructive feedback.

Moreover, ongoing education and training on topics such as cultural competence, communication skills, and conflict resolution can help health-care professionals navigate challenging interpersonal dynamics and promote supportive and inclusive work environments.

Ultimately, by acknowledging and addressing the complexities of power dynamics in health-care settings, we can work toward building healthier, more equitable workplaces where all members of the health-care team feel valued, respected, and empowered to provide the best possible care for their patients.

The power dynamics and hierarchical structures within corporate medical environments can sometimes mirror the oppressive systems of the past, evoking memories of slavery and subjugation. Just as slaves were expected to unquestioningly obey their masters or face punishment, physicians may feel compelled to comply with directives from higher-ups in the health-care hierarchy, even if those directives undermine their autonomy or professional judgment.

Despite the flaws and shortcomings of our health-care system, particularly within correctional facilities, it is worth noting that jails and prisons are among the few places where people are guaranteed access to health care. Laws mandate that inmates receive both physical and mental health care, and failure to provide adequate care can result in significant legal consequences.

However, the quality of care in correctional settings varies widely, and many do not receive the level of care they need or deserve. Limited resources, understaffing, and systemic barriers contribute to gaps in care, particularly for marginalized populations such as Black inmates.

Addressing these issues requires a many-sided approach that prioritizes the health and well-being of all, regardless of their incarceration status. This includes advocating for comprehensive health-care policies, increasing funding for health-care services, addressing systemic inequalities that disproportionately affect marginalized communities, and promoting cultural competence and sensitivity among health-care providers.

Ultimately, ensuring access to quality health care, both inside and outside correctional facilities, is essential to upholding basic human rights and promoting health equity. It requires a collective effort to dismantle oppressive systems and create a more just and compassionate health-care system for everyone.

The landscape of health care has undergone significant transformation, with profound implications for the doctor–patient relationship and the delivery of medical services. While efforts like those of President Obama aimed to expand access to health care and ensure coverage for all, the reality is that the practice of medicine has become increasingly entangled with business interests and insurance reimbursement models.

The introduction of concepts like "relative value scale," which determines physician payment based on the complexity of treatments and severity of conditions, was initially intended to standardize compensation and to ensure fair reimbursement. However, the integration of medicine into a business model within a capitalistic society has led to unintended consequences.

Today, doctors find themselves navigating a complex web of relationships involving not just patients, but also insurance companies and payers. The rise of preferred provider organizations (PPOs) and health maintenance organizations (HMOs) has further complicated matters, with physicians often beholden to the dictates and reimbursement rates set by these entities.

As a result, the traditional doctor–patient relationship, once characterized by trust, empathy, and personalized care, has been eroded by external pressures and financial considerations. Physicians may find themselves constrained by bureaucratic red tape, incentivized to prioritize cost containment over patient well-being, and subject to metrics and quotas that prioritize profitability over quality of care.

In this increasingly commercialized landscape, the fundamental principles of medicine, including the Hippocratic oath to prioritize patient welfare above all else, can sometimes feel like relics of a bygone era. Yet, amid these challenges, there remains a pressing need to advocate for policies and practices that prioritize human dignity, equitable access to care, and the sanctity of the doctor–patient relationship.

The intersection of profit motives and health care, both within the broader medical industry and specifically within the context of incarceration, raises profound ethical and societal concerns. The commodification of health care, with companies on the stock market profiting from that care, reflects a troubling trend in which financial gain takes precedence over patient well- being.

Similarly, the for-profit prison system, where companies profit from incarcerating individuals, perpetuates systemic inequalities and creates echoes of historical injustices such as slavery. The profit-driven model incentivizes higher rates of incarceration, particularly among marginalized communities, which are disproportionately impacted by poverty and systemic racism.

Michelle Alexander's seminal work, The New Jim Crow, sheds light on how the criminal justice system perpetuates racial oppression and mass incarceration, disproportionately affecting Black communities. The parallels between historical injustices and contemporary practices underscore the urgent need for systemic reform and social justice advocacy.

As Black physicians, it is crucial for us to be cognizant of our history and the legacy of exploitation and discrimination that has shaped our health-care system. We must advocate for patient autonomy, informed consent, and equitable access to care, resisting systems that prioritize profit over human dignity and well-being. By acknowledging our past and actively working toward a more just and equitable future, we can strive to uphold the principles of ethical health care and social justice for all.

The power vested in physicians, particularly psychiatrists, to involuntarily hospitalize individuals who pose a threat to themselves or others is a weighty responsibility that must be wielded with the utmost care and integrity. This authority, while essential for ensuring public safety and providing necessary treatment to those in crisis, also carries significant ethical considerations.

Psychiatrists are uniquely positioned to assess patients' mental health and to make critical decisions regarding their care, including the decision to involuntarily hospitalize them. This authority is granted based on the understanding that individuals experiencing severe mental illness may lack insight into their condition and may be unable to make rational decisions about their own safety or the safety of others.

However, with this power comes a profound obligation to uphold the principles of dignity, respect, and compassion for the patient. It is essential that psychiatrists approach the decision to involuntarily hospitalize someone with empathy, understanding, and a commitment to preserving the person's autonomy to the greatest extent possible.

71

Furthermore, it is imperative for psychiatrists to carefully consider the potential impact of involuntary hospitalization on patients' well-being and to ensure that all efforts are made to provide appropriate treatment and support during their hospitalization. This includes involving patients in treatment decisions to the extent possible and respecting their wishes whenever feasible.

Ultimately, the power to involuntarily hospitalize should be exercised judiciously, with a focus on promoting the best interests of patients and safeguarding their rights and dignity. It is a solemn responsibility that requires a balance of compassion, clinical expertise, and ethical integrity to ensure that individuals receive the care and support they need while respecting their autonomy and human rights.

As Black physicians, we are acutely aware of the historical injustices and atrocities that people of color have endured, including slavery, systemic racism, and acts of violence and discrimination. The derogatory terms and dehumanizing treatment inflicted on Black people throughout history serve as painful reminders of the profound impact of racism and oppression on our communities.

In the face of such injustices, it is essential to recognize that as physicians and as human beings, we answer to a higher authority: Almighty God. Regardless of our race, ethnicity, or background, we are all accountable for our actions and decisions, and we are called to uphold the principles of justice, compassion, and integrity in our interactions with others.

By adopting the mindset of the humanity of others, rather than by merely treating them, we affirm our commitment to providing holistic, patient-centered care that respects the inherent dignity and worth of everyone. This approach reflects our belief in the sanctity of human life and our recognition of the divine mandate to love and care for one another as children of God.

In light of this awareness, I make it a point to address the individuals I care for as Mr. or Mrs., acknowledging the significance of their title and affirming their inherent worth and value as human beings. This simple yet meaningful gesture reflects my commitment to honoring the humanity and dignity of each person I encounter.

Even in environments where individuals may be dehumanized or reduced to numbers, such as in correctional facilities, I believe it is essential to uphold the dignity of every person by addressing them with the respect they deserve. By doing so, I seek to counteract the dehumanizing effects of institutionalization and affirm the humanity of those in my care.

The initial interaction between a medical caretaker and a patient sets the foundation for the entire health-care journey. It is during this crucial moment that trust is established, concerns are addressed, and a sense of mutual respect and understanding is cultivated.

As a medical caretaker, I recognize the significance of the first interaction and strive to approach it with empathy, compassion, and attentiveness, as it sets the tone for the doctor-patient relationship. My goal is to create a welcoming and supportive environment where patients feel heard, valued, and respected. During this initial encounter, I actively listen to the patient's concerns, preferences, and health goals. I ask open-ended questions to gain a comprehensive understanding of their medical history, symptoms, and lifestyle factors that may impact their health.

Building rapport, earning trust and establishing a strong therapeutic alliance is essential for effective health-care delivery. Along with addressing immediate medical needs, I prioritize creating a supportive and trusting relationship with my patients. Clear and effective communication is key to fostering this alliance. I make sure to use language that is easily understandable and free of medical jargon, ensuring that patients can fully comprehend their diagnosis, treatment options, and health-care plan. By communicating in a transparent and accessible manner, I empower patients to actively engage in their own care and make informed decisions about their health.

Through open and transparent communication, I always encourage patients to voice their concerns, preferences, and goals, ensuring that their individual needs and values are central to the decision-making process. By actively involving patients in health-care decisions, we can tailor treatment plans to align with their unique circumstances and empower them to make informed choices about their health.

Furthermore, fostering a positive and trusting relationship from the outset promotes patient engagement and adherence to treatment recommendations. When patients feel seen, respected, heard, and valued, they are more likely to actively participate in their care, follow through with prescribed interventions, and adopt healthy behaviors that contribute to better health outcomes.

Ultimately, by prioritizing patient-centered care and building a collaborative partnership, we can work together to achieve optimal health and well-being for each individual, leading to improved quality of life and overall satisfaction with health-care experiences.

Chapter 8: Why Did I Choose Psychiatry?

The decision to pursue a career in psychiatry is deeply personal and multidimensional, shaped by a combination of experiences, values, and aspirations. For me, the decision was influenced by a variety of factors, each contributing to my passion for mental health and my desire to make a meaningful difference in people's lives.

From as young as I can remember until the eighth grade, I grew up in Liberty City. My parents were both considered middle class, such as middle class was for Black people. Indeed, for Black people coming out of the racist South, it was quite an accomplishment for both of them. My dad actually spent two years at Florida A&M College and was drafted into the Army in his second year. He reached the rank of sergeant. He seldom talked about his experiences in the Army, and after watching many war films and documentaries, I could see why. His Army experience did help him train to be a great protector and fierce in his approach to life. My mother graduated from Florida A&M College, she was a home economics major and became a school teacher. She taught at Dorsey High School, which eventually became a middle school and is now a technical school.

I am sure that my father's experiences in the Army changed his outlook on life. Upon his return to the United States, he completed his pharmacy degree at Xavier University in New Orleans. He eventually came to own three drugstores with a partner whom he met in pharmacy school, my godfather, Samuel Johnson Sr.

Both my sister and I attended Catholic school because, having gone to Xavier, a Catholic school, probably converted my father to that religion. We attended Holy Redeemer Catholic School, which was in the inner city and has since closed.

Being seen as "rich kids," I was the one who bore the brunt of jokes and intimidation by my peers—what we would call bullying today. One way I tried to assimilate was to play every sport I could; I excelled at two—basketball and golf.

My parents made sure that my education took priority over everything else. I remember them walking me into one of my teacher's classroom at a young age, much to the delight of onlookers, and chastising me about my less than stellar work performance. Boy, was I embarrassed. I think that was the only time I had to accompany my parents to see a teacher for the rest of my primary and high school years. To my sister's and my benefit, they expected and demanded academic success from both of us, and as the older child I had to set the standard.

The education provided by the nuns and female lay teachers was truly excellent. In fact, my introduction to algebra began as early as sixth grade. We had what I've always affectionately referred to as "telemath." Interestingly, the prefix "tele-" is quite popular now, but looking back, the concept was introduced to me when I was just eleven years old. We would gather to watch a White gentleman teach us algebra through televised lessons. It took me three years to fully grasp the concept that, in algebra, a letter represents a number. This early exposure played a pivotal role in my academic journey and subsequent advancement through the educational system.

Returning to the topic of sports, it's worth noting that one common pathway to assimilation among Black men growing up in the "hood," a phenomenon that persists to this day, is through participation in sports. In my case, basketball was the arena where I truly shone during my elementary school years. With each passing year, my skills improved. By the time I reached the eighth grade, our team was regularly scoring a hundred points per game. Although I played on the junior varsity team in high school, I didn't progress to varsity level.

76

The high school I attended, Archbishop Curley, was renowned for its basketball team during my formative grade school years. It was a time when the local sports scene buzzed with the legend of Cyril Baptiste, one of the earliest basketball prodigies to emerge from Miami. Cyril, standing an impressive six feet, eight inches, cast a towering shadow over his peers on the court. His prowess and leadership propelled our school to an undefeated season during his senior year, a feat that captured the imagination of our community. We were so confident in the team's abilities that we had already hailed them as state champions before they even stepped onto the court for the district playoffs.

However, amid our fervor and local triumphs, we remained unaware of a smaller school located seemingly a world away, though just a mere four-hour drive by car. This school, tucked in another corner of the state, would soon emerge as an unexpected challenger, altering the course of our basketball narrative.

The game was broadcast over the radio; we listened to it at home. I did not get the full impact until the next morning when I flipped to the sports section of the paper as I usually did. Some kid from Key West caught a length of the floor pass over young Cyril and broke a tie along with every little boy's heart in the eighth grade at Holy Redeemer. His name was Ronald Harris, better known as Dr. Ronald Harris, who went on to play at Florida State, which won the NCAA championship while he was on the squad. Ronald would eventually go on to obtain his medical degree. Baptiste went on to play at Creighton in Nebraska, but eventually fell on hard times.

Dr. Harris' journey to Miami to practice family medicine symbolizes the culmination of years of dedication and hard work. The demanding schedule both of athletic pursuits and academic endeavors is a testament to his perseverance and determination. Similarly, Dr. Myron Rolle's remarkable achievements on the football field and in the operating room as a neurosurgeon serve as a reminder of the boundless potential that exists in our communities.

As we navigate through life, it becomes evident that true role models are not distant idols but individuals who walk among us every day. They are the teachers who ignite passion in their students, the bus drivers who ensure safe passage to school, and the health-care workers who tirelessly care for the sick. Moreover, the valor exhibited by law enforcement personnel, who bravely confront danger to uphold the law, deserves our utmost respect and admiration.

In reflecting on my own upbringing, I recognize the significance of the challenges I faced and the resilience I developed in overcoming them. Today, as conversations around mental health gain momentum, it is essential to acknowledge and address the traumas of our past while also celebrating the strength and resilience that define our journeys.

The echoes of my childhood experiences reverberate through my adult life, particularly in the realm of sleep. Growing up in Liberty City, a community on the brink of devastation due to the impending cocaine epidemic, instilled in me a sense of vigilance and unease. While my father's decision to relocate our family likely saved my life, the haunting memories of friends lost to the streets linger with me to date.

The nightly symphony of sounds that emanated from the alley behind our home served as a constant reminder of the harsh realities of our environment. From the visceral sounds of altercations to the intimate yet unsettling encounters of strangers, the alley painted a vivid tableau of urban life. Each night, I lay awake, my senses heightened by the harshness outside my window.

However, one particular night stands out from the chaos. The chilling screams of a man in distress pierced the darkness, sending shivers down my spine. With each blow, I felt his pain as if it were my own. The desperate pleas for mercy echoed in the stillness of the night, leaving an indelible mark on my psyche.

As the turmoil unfolded, my parents were abruptly awakened, their instincts honed by years of navigating the dangers of our neighborhood. Armed with nothing but his military pistol and a steely resolve, my father ventured into the night, determined to confront the source of the chaos. Despite my mother's trepidation, he knew the gravity of the situation demanded action. He was just that kind of man. My father fired several warning shots to end the brutal assault that caused the assaulter to flee, giving the victim a second chance.

In the aftermath of that fateful night, as the echoes of gunfire faded into the distance, a sense of relief washed over our household. Yet the memory of that harrowing experience lingered, a stark reminder of the fragility of life in our community.

In recounting this tale to a close friend, who was White, I was struck by the profound contrast between our experiences. For him, the notion of gunshots outside of a controlled environment was unfathomable and only reserved for gun ranges, highlighting the gaping chasm between our worlds.

Indeed, the disparities between Black and lower socioeconomic communities and their affluent counterparts are stark and deeply entrenched. What is accepted as normalcy in one context reveals the pervasive inequality that plagues our society.

Psychiatry is a field that continuously evolves as new research advances our understanding of the brain and behavior. I was inspired by the opportunity for lifelong learning and professional growth offered by psychiatry, knowing that I would have the chance to engage in ongoing education, research, and clinical practice to enhance my skills and knowledge.

My decision to pursue psychiatry was driven by a combination of personal experiences, social consciousness, academic interests, and a commitment to holistic, patient-centered care. As a psychiatrist, I am dedicated to promoting mental health equity, advocating for marginalized communities, and supporting individuals on their journey toward healing and recovery.

Medical school is undeniably challenging, demanding dedication, perseverance, and a readiness to make significant sacrifices in pursuit of one's goals. The rigors of medical education are particularly evident in the length and intensity of specialty training, with some fields requiring an extensive commitment of time and effort.

Surgery, in particular, stands out as one of the most demanding specialties, with training programs typically lasting eight years or longer. This extended duration reflects the complexity and depth of knowledge required to excel in surgical practice. Aspiring surgeons must possess exceptional surgical skills, critical thinking abilities, and a profound understanding of anatomy, physiology, and pathology.

The journey to becoming a surgeon involves not only rigorous academic coursework but also extensive hands-on training in operating rooms, clinics, and hospital settings. Trainees must navigate challenging rotations, long hours, and high-pressure situations, all while balancing their academic pursuits with personal and professional responsibilities.

The commitment required for surgical training extends far beyond the confines of medical school, encompassing years of residency and fellowship training, as well as ongoing continuing education throughout one's career. This dedication is essential to ensure that surgeons are equipped to provide safe, effective, and compassionate care to their patients.

While the path to becoming a surgeon is undeniably arduous, it is also deeply rewarding for those who are passionate about the field. The opportunity to make a meaningful difference in the lives of patients, to innovate and advance surgical techniques, and to contribute to the collective body of medical knowledge makes the sacrifices of surgical training worthwhile.

Indeed, the demanding nature of surgical training results in a relatively smaller number of surgeons compared to physicians specializing in fields such as general medicine, family medicine, pediatrics, or psychiatry. The scarcity of surgeons reflects the extensive commitment required to acquire the necessary skills and expertise.

Compensation in the medical field typically corresponds to the level of complexity and specialization of the chosen specialty. Surgeons, given the intricate nature of their work and the extensive training involved, often command higher salaries compared to their counterparts in other medical disciplines. This financial reward serves as recognition of the significant investment of time, effort, and resources required to become proficient in surgery.

Likewise, different medical specialties demand specific qualities and attributes from practitioners. For instance, surgery necessitates not only a high level of manual dexterity but also a strong stomach and a willingness to work in environments where blood and bodily tissue are commonplace. Surgeons must possess the ability to remain calm under pressure, make quick and accurate decisions, and maintain focus and precision during complex procedures.

These unique qualities and demands inherent in surgical practice set it apart from other medical specialties and attract individuals who are drawn to the challenges and rewards of surgical care.

While surgery may not be suitable for everyone, those who possess the requisite skills, temperament, and passion for the field find fulfillment and satisfaction in the opportunity to make a salutary impact on the lives of their patients through surgical intervention.

General medicine, also known as internal medicine, is among the most common medical specialties, along with family and pediatric medicine. Unlike surgical fields, general medicine typically does not require the same level of manual dexterity. Neurology, another specialty closely related to psychiatry, involves a hands-on approach, and requires a deep understanding of the brain, similar to psychiatry.

Psychiatry holds a distinct place among medical specialties. While it may not demand the same intensity as surgical or internal medicine fields, it is nonetheless vital. Many women choose psychiatry because it offers a slightly less demanding workload while still providing meaningful patient care. Despite being less demanding, psychiatry is no less important in the medical landscape.

Students who pursue psychiatry often exhibit qualities such as passion, compassion, and a genuine enjoyment of working with people. Some may have personal experiences with psychiatric illness, either themselves or within their families. Importantly, being diagnosed with a psychiatric condition does not necessarily preclude someone from pursuing a career in medicine. However, individuals with major mental disorders must prioritize medication compliance, stress management, and adequate support.

In fact, those with conditions like bipolar disorder, characterized by periods of hyperactivity and grandiosity, may find certain aspects of medical training appealing, particularly

82

during periods of remission. With proper management, these people can excel in medical school and go on to become successful psychiatrists, leveraging their unique insights and experiences to provide compassionate care to others.

Many successful people indeed struggle with bipolar disorder, leveraging their unique experiences to excel in various disciplines and contribute significantly to their fields. The ability to maintain high levels of productivity and dedication, even during periods of heightened activity, can be a hallmark of those with bipolar disorder.

In the field of psychiatry, compassion, empathy, understanding, and non-judgment are fundamental qualities expected of practitioners. Patients should feel supported and valued by their psychiatrists, and if these qualities are lacking, it is crucial to seek care elsewhere. Unfortunately, there is a shortage of psychiatrists, particularly among minority communities. In Florida alone, with a population of approximately twenty-two million, the scarcity of psychiatrists is evident, compounded by the fact that only 1 percent of psychiatrists in America are Black.

The prevalence of mental illness within the criminal justice system is alarming, with jails and prisons effectively becoming the new asylums. Rates of schizophrenia and suicide inside these institutions far surpass those in the general population, in which suicide, in particular, remains a significant concern, ranking among the leading causes of death for both adults and children.

Contrary to misconceptions, suicide affects all races, including Black communities. Despite prevailing stereotypes suggesting resilience, Black people are not immune to mental illness or suicidal ideation. Some mistakenly perceive mental health struggles as a sign of weakness, perpetuating harmful stigma and preventing individuals from seeking help. However, acknowledging and addressing mental health issues within

Black communities is crucial for promoting overall well-being and reducing the devastating impact of suicide.

For example, the alarming increase in the Black adolescent suicide rate reveals an urgent need to address mental health care barriers immediately. Newly reported data from the Centers for Disease Control and Prevention's (CDC's) WONDER database on February 5, 2024, has highlighted a concerning trend. From 2018 to 2022, Black adolescent suicides have increased by 54%, surpassing the suicide rate of their White peers for the first time in 2022, while the suicide rate for White youth decreased by 17% during the same period. The suicide rate among Black adolescents is rising faster than any other racial or ethnic group. From 2007 to 2020, the suicide rate among Black youth aged 10 to 17 rose by 144%. Despite the overall downward trend in youth suicide rates, this data emphasizes the urgent necessity to enhance mental health care for Black communities.

Black adolescents face significant barriers to accessing mental health care compared to their peers in other demographic groups. These obstacles stem from systemic inequities such as racism and poverty, as well as pervasive stigma surrounding mental health and a justified cultural mistrust of the healthcare system. These factors combine to create substantial challenges in obtaining quality mental health resources for this group.

Indeed, the functioning of the human brain transcends racial boundaries, with brain chemistry imbalances affecting individuals of all ethnic backgrounds. This truth was underscored by an affecting moment during my general anatomy class, where a classmate, Dr. Douglas Nalls, asked a thought- provoking question.

Dr. Nalls, who tragically succumbed to chronic kidney disease—an ailment disproportionately affecting Black people due to complications from diabetes and hypertension—challenged our understanding of racial disparities in anatomy.

While I attended a predominantly Black institution, Dr. Nalls attended an Ivy League college in the North, where he excelled. He was able to demonstrate his proficiency and knowledge with certain courses like biochemistry by standardized testing that allowed him to gain immediate credit for various subject areas rather than attending class in a traditional classroom setting for course completion. The College-Level Examination Program (CLEP) is a series of tests you can take to earn college credit for your degree, rather than sitting in a classroom for a full semester.

During a lecture, Dr. Nalls asked my anatomy professor whether there were any anatomical differences between white and black bodies. The response was a resounding "No." This exchange underscored the universality of human anatomy, highlighting that beneath our outward differences, our internal structures remain fundamentally the same. Dr. Nall's powerful reminder that biology knows no racial boundaries challenged preconceived notions and fostered a deeper appreciation for the inherent similarities that bind us all as human beings.

The experience of dissecting cadavers during medical school was a profound one, offering invaluable insights into the intricacies of human anatomy. Despite the racial diversity among the cadavers we encountered, a striking similarity emerged: the organs, regardless of the person's race, exhibited remarkable uniformity in size and positioning inside the body. Even the structure of the brain, often considered the seat of mental processes, displayed consistency in size across different racial groups.

This tangible demonstration of anatomical similarity dispels any notion that certain races are immune to mental disorders. Instead, it underscores the universal nature of these conditions, which are rooted in the complex workings of the brain. While genetic and biological factors undoubtedly contribute to the development of mental illness, environmental influences and behavioral patterns can also impact brain function.

Acknowledging this reality is crucial in dismantling misconceptions and stereotypes surrounding mental health within the Black community. By recognizing that mental disorders are not exclusive to any particular race, we can foster greater understanding and empathy for those struggling with these conditions. Moreover, it highlights the importance of addressing social determinants of health and promoting mental wellness through holistic approaches that consider both biological and environmental factors.

Ultimately, this realization serves as a powerful reminder of our shared humanity and the need for inclusive and equitable mental health care for all, regardless of race or ethnicity. By embracing diversity and cultural competence in our approach to mental health, we can strive toward creating a more compassionate and supportive society for everyone.

The stark contrast between the pristine, authoritative environment of traditional medical practice and the complex, adversarial nature of correctional settings highlights the unique challenges faced by psychiatrists working in jails and prisons. Unlike the controlled atmosphere of a clinic or hospital, where patients seek treatment voluntarily, the criminal justice system operates within an inherently adversarial framework.

Inmates, by virtue of their confinement, have typically violated societal norms and laws. In this context, the dynamics of power and authority are markedly different from those encountered in traditional medical practice. Rather than being greeted with respect and deference, health-care providers in correctional facilities may encounter hostility, skepticism, or resistance from inmates who are distrustful of authority figures.

Moreover, the coercive nature of the correctional system presents ethical dilemmas for psychiatrists, who must navigate the tension between upholding their duty to provide compassionate, patient-centered care and adhering to institutional policies and security protocols. This dynamic can challenge the principles of autonomy and informed consent, as patients may feel compelled to comply with treatment recommendations due to the constraints of their confinement.

Despite these challenges, the need for psychiatrists in correctional settings, particularly those from diverse backgrounds, is undeniable. The prevalence of mental illness among incarcerated populations is disproportionately high, and access to mental-health-care services is often limited. Black psychiatrists, in particular, bring valuable cultural competence and insights into the unique experiences and challenges faced by Black inmates.

By advocating for greater diversity in the psychiatric workforce and promoting culturally responsive care in correctional settings, we can strive to address the mental health needs of inmates more effectively. This requires a commitment to equity, compassion, and social justice, as well as an acknowledgment of the systemic barriers and injustices that perpetuate disparities in mental-health-care access and potential outcomes.

For most physicians, the courtroom is a foreign and anxiety-inducing environment, far removed from the familiar settings of offices and hospitals where they typically practice medicine. Stepping into a courtroom, whether as a witness or defendant, can evoke feelings of intimidation and discomfort, especially for those unaccustomed to legal proceedings.

The courtroom setting, with its formalities, rules, and decorum, can be particularly daunting for those facing criminal charges. For many, the experience of being involved in a legal case is unfamiliar and carries with it a sense of shame or embarrassment. Despite the prevalence of media portrayals glamorizing criminal behavior, the reality of being entangled in the legal system is far from glamorous.

In today's digital age, there is a concerning trend among younger generations to view encounters with the law as badges of honor or symbols of toughness. This misguided perception, often fueled by media and social influences, trivializes the serious consequences of criminal behavior, and overlooks the harsh realities of incarceration.

In truth, the experience of being incarcerated is anything but glamorous. It involves loss of freedom, separation from loved ones, and exposure to potentially dangerous or degrading conditions. For those facing criminal charges, appearing in court is a reminder of the serious implications of their actions and of the need to navigate a legal system that can be unforgiving and complex.

As physicians, it is essential to recognize the profound impact that involvement in the legal system can have on one's physical and mental well-being. By offering support, understanding, and nonjudgmental care to patients who have encountered legal troubles, health-care providers can play a vital role in helping them navigate the challenges they face and work toward rehabilitation and recovery.

Jails and prisons have historically been institutions designed to exert control, punish, and deter undesirable behaviors. Rather than focusing on rehabilitation and support, these facilities have often prioritized punishment and discipline. They are typically characterized by strict regulations, limited freedoms, and harsh conditions, all of which contribute to the dehumanization of inmates. This punitive approach to justice has led to the development of systems that prioritize punishment over rehabilitation, resulting in high rates of recidivism and perpetuating cycles of incarceration.

The conditions in jails and prisons are often substandard, with overcrowding, inadequate health care, and limited access to education and rehabilitation programs. These conditions can further contribute to the dehumanization of inmates, stripping them of their dignity, autonomy, and sense of self-worth.

Overall, jails and prisons have historically served as negative reinforcements of human behavior, perpetuating cycles of punishment and retribution rather than addressing the underlying causes of criminality and promoting rehabilitation and social reintegration. Recognizing the inherent dehumanization within these systems is essential for advocating for reforms that prioritize human rights, dignity, and well-being, both inside and outside correctional facilities.

Forensic psychiatrists hold a unique and prestigious position within the field of psychiatry. While plastic surgeons may be considered the "golden boys" of medicine due to their perceived glamour and high-profile clientele, forensic psychiatrists are revered within the realm of psychiatry for their expertise in legal matters and courtroom testimony.

These specialized psychiatrists are often called upon to provide expert opinions and evaluations in legal cases involving mental health issues. They play a crucial role in assessing the mental state of defendants, providing insights into their behavior and motivations and offering recommendations for legal proceedings on competency to stand trial and insanity pleas.

Testifying in court as an expert witness requires a forensic psychiatrist to convey complex psychiatric concepts in a clear and compelling manner to judges, lawyers, and juries. Their testimony can have significant implications for the outcome, making their role both challenging and influential.
In high-profile cases, forensic psychiatrists may garner widespread attention from the media and the public. Their insights and opinions may be dissected and debated in the public sphere, further highlighting the importance of their expertise in understanding the intersection of mental health and the law.

Dr. Park Dietz, based in California, is renowned for his work as a forensic psychiatrist. His contributions to high-profile cases and his expertise in forensic psychiatry have solidified his reputation as a leading authority in the field.

Forensic psychiatrists occupy a pivotal role at the joining of mental health and the legal system. Their expertise is not only valued by the psychiatric community but also recognized and sought after by the legal professionals, judges, and law enforcement agencies.

One of the key responsibilities of forensic psychiatrists is to conduct thorough evaluations of defendants, witnesses, and victims. These evaluations may encompass a wide range of psychiatric assessments, such as determining competency to stand trial, assessing mental state at the time of the offense, evaluating the presence of mental disorders, and gauging the risk of future dangerousness.

Forensic psychiatrists may also play a crucial role in shaping public policy and legal standards related to mental health. Through their involvement in landmark cases and their contributions to the development of legal precedents, they help establish guidelines and protocols for addressing mental health issues within the criminal justice system.

Furthermore, forensic psychiatrists may be called on to consult and guide various stakeholders, including attorneys, law enforcement agencies, correctional facilities, and mental health professionals. Their expertise extends beyond the courtroom, encompassing a broad range of forensic settings and scenarios where mental health intersects with the law. Thus, forensic psychiatrists occupy a unique and varied role that requires a deep understanding of both psychiatric principles and legal processes. Their work is instrumental in ensuring that individuals with mental health issues are treated fairly and equitably by the legal system, and their contributions have far-reaching implications for both individual cases and broader societal norms.

During my psychiatry residency, I had my initial exposure to the jail and prison environment, where I encountered a remarkable mentor, Dr. Sanford Jacobson, and Dr. Barry Morris, who hired me to work in the jail. Dr. Jacobson was widely recognized in Miami-Dade County for his expertise in forensic psychiatry and was often called upon to provide expert testimony on mental health issues. Dr. Robert Bragg, a distinguished Black psychiatrist at the University of Miami Miller School of Medicine, played a pivotal role in promoting diversity within the field of psychiatry, actively recruiting Black students and establishing scholarships for them.

What struck me about Dr. Jacobson was his fearlessness in tackling the challenges of the Miami-Dade County jail system. His willingness to navigate imposing steel gates and confront the harsh realities of incarceration, particularly among young Black inmates, spoke volumes about his character and commitment to serving marginalized communities. This experience underscored psychiatry's transformative potential in addressing societal inequalities and advocating for mental well- being, regardless of circumstances.

During my psychiatry residency, Dr. Jacobson's dedication made a profound impression on me. His reputation as a respected expert in forensic psychiatry and his frequent involvement in court proceedings demonstrated his commitment to ensuring mental health considerations were appropriately addressed.

Additionally, Dr. Robert Bragg's influential presence at the University of Miami Miller School of Medicine emphasized the importance of diversity and inclusion in psychiatry. His efforts to recruit and support Black students, along with his prestigious background in psychiatry, inspired aspiring Black professionals in the field.

Yet, it was Dr. Jacobson's courage to enter the challenging environment of the Miami-Dade County jail system that truly resonated with me. The compassion required to engage with incarcerated individuals, especially young Black individuals facing systemic challenges, reflected his unwavering commitment to providing mental health care to those in need, regardless of the setting.

Dr. Jacobson's example reminded me of the importance of stepping outside one's comfort zone and confronting the realities of marginalized communities. It reinforced that effective psychiatric care extends beyond clinical settings and requires active engagement with overlooked or underserved populations. His actions exemplified psychiatry's potential to address social injustices and advocate for the mental well-being of all, regardless of circumstances.

Working in jails and prisons held a unique allure for me as I embarked on my career path. There was an undeniable sense of excitement and significance in the prospect of being involved in high-profile criminal cases, potentially appearing on TV or having my name featured in newspapers. While the prospect of media exposure was appealing, I recognized that the real value lay in the opportunity to serve those who were most in need of mental health support.

In the correctional system, I saw a population that was often overlooked and underserved—the marginalized, the minorities, and the young men who represented the future of our community and our nation. It was a chance to make a meaningful impact in the lives of those who faced immense challenges and barriers to accessing mental-health care. This calling stirred within me a sense of purpose and drive to advocate for those who were often voiceless and ignored.

Despite the difficulties and hardships that came with the territory, I was drawn to the profound sense of fulfillment that came from serving this population and making a difference in their lives.

My parents, like countless others, had a traditional view of what constitutes a "real" doctor, and unfortunately, they didn't perceive psychiatry as fitting that mold. Despite their reservations, if I were given the chance to start over, I would still choose the path of becoming a psychiatrist without hesitation.

Why, you may ask? Because we are currently witnessing an unprecedented era of advancements in the field, particularly in our understanding of the brain and the development of innovative treatments. From groundbreaking discoveries in neurobiology to the introduction of novel therapeutic interventions, psychiatry is at the forefront of medical progress.

Take, for instance, the recent breakthroughs in pharmacotherapy. We now have nasal spray formulations designed to alleviate symptoms of depression rapidly, providing much-needed relief for patients who may have struggled with conventional treatments. Additionally, the introduction of long-acting medications for conditions like schizophrenia offers a significant improvement in patient care by ensuring consistent and sustained drug delivery, thereby reducing the burden of frequent dosing.

Another notable advancement lies in the management of bipolar disorder. Thanks to the development of new medications that no longer necessitate rigorous blood monitoring, patients can experience greater autonomy in their treatment journey while still receiving effective care. This represents a monumental shift in how we approach and address mental health conditions, fostering a more patient-centered and accessible health-care landscape.

Indeed, the current landscape of psychiatry is characterized by unparalleled opportunities for practitioners and patients alike. As we continue to unravel the complexities of the human mind and refine our therapeutic strategies, the future of psychiatry appears incredibly promising. It is not just a profession; it is a gateway to transformative change and improved quality of life for countless individuals. There has never been a better time to be a psychiatrist.

Chapter 9: The Nature of Incarceration and Support Structures

In this chapter, we consider the intricate dynamics of incarceration and the support systems surrounding it. From personal anecdotes to professional insights, we explore the multiple challenges encountered by individuals navigating the criminal justice system while wrestling with mental health issues. This chapter is not merely an examination of challenges but a call to action.

Through grassroots advocacy and community partnerships, we uncover avenues for change. By amplifying the voices of those impacted and advocating for equitable access to mental health resources, we strive to dismantle the oppressive structures that perpetuate cycles of incarceration and despair. As we navigate the complexities of incarceration and its surrounding support systems, we are reminded of the resilience and strength inherent in communities. This chapter serves as a testament to the transformative power of psychiatry to heal, empower, and inspire change, even within the most challenging of circumstances.

Through expressive narratives and thought-provoking analysis, we uncover the systemic barriers that disproportionately affect marginalized communities, particularly Black and Brown.

From inadequate access to mental health services to the stigma surrounding mental illness in the criminal justice system, we confront the harsh realities that demand urgent attention and reform.

But amid these challenges shines a beacon of hope. Through grassroots advocacy, community partnerships, and innovative interventions, we discover the potential for positive change.

The ninth floor of the Miami-Dade Detention Center earned the ominous moniker, the "Forgotten Floor." For decades, away from public scrutiny, this floor became a harrowing site where inmates, many of whom suffered from severe mental illnesses and were often charged with minor offenses, found themselves detained for extended periods, sometimes spanning months or even years.

Throughout the majority of my career, I've dedicated myself to both salaried positions and maintaining a private practice. It all began with my first salaried position at South Florida State Hospital, where I immersed myself in providing care for people with chronic mental illness. This experience lasted approximately eighteen months and laid the foundation for my journey in psychiatric medicine.

Following my tenure at South Florida State Hospital, I transitioned to a role at the Forensic Hospital, which catered to the needs of residents of the southern region of Florida. Specifically, I worked at the South Florida Evaluation Treatment Center in Miami, which was one of several state-run forensic psychiatric hospitals in Florida. In addition to the Miami facility, there were the North Florida Evaluation Treatment Center serving the northern part of the state, Arcadia State Hospital covering the western region, and the renowned Florida State Hospital located in Chattahoochee.

Each of these institutions played a vital role in providing mental health services in Florida, with a particular focus on forensic psychiatry—addressing the intersection of mental health and the criminal justice system. My time at these facilities yielded invaluable insights and shaped my approach to psychiatric practice, especially in navigating the complexities of treating individuals within forensic settings.

The Hospital System

The landscape of the forensic hospital system in Florida has indeed evolved over time, but the core mission remains consistent: to assist individuals with mental illness who are not yet fit to stand trial or to treat those declared not guilty by reason of insanity. Those adjudicated not guilty by reason of insanity are relatively few in number.

One of the critical standards adopted by federal courts, which Florida treatment providers adhere to, is ensuring that individuals possess the capacity to communicate effectively with their legal counsel and comprehend the charges against them.

When I initially joined the team at the South Florida Evaluation Treatment Center, we encountered a diverse range of cases, from minor offenses like loitering to more serious crimes like murder. Our primary responsibility as treatment teams was to work toward restoring these offenders to competency, particularly those struggling with severe mental illnesses like schizophrenia.

In accordance with the mandate set forth by the United States Supreme Court, it is imperative that individuals facing legal proceedings have the fundamental ability to communicate rationally with their attorney and comprehend the charges levied against them. In Dusky v. United States (1960), the Supreme Court determined that an individual must be able to rationally understand the trial proceedings and consult with their lawyer to be considered mentally competent for trial. This principle, enshrined in the Sixth Amendment to the United States Constitution, guarantees the right to counsel and ensures a fair trial for all defendants. Thus, my commitment to facilitating effective communication and understanding aligns seamlessly with this constitutional imperative. Throughout my professional experience, I have upheld the principles of clear and coherent communication, ensuring that all parties comprehend the complexities of related legal matters.

97

Fostering an environment of open dialogue and transparency enables people to meaningfully engage in legal proceedings, empowering them to fully participate in their own defense.

Navigating Landmines

Many of the inmates we encountered had either not been identified as mentally ill during their time in jail or had not received treatment to stabilize their condition. As a result, they found themselves unable to engage with the legal process effectively. Our goal was to intervene, providing comprehensive treatment to address their mental health needs and equip them with the capacity to participate in their legal proceedings.

However, the sheer volume of mentally ill individuals often led to significant backlogs in cases awaiting resolution. In some instances, the pressure to expedite the process resulted in people being returned to court prematurely before they had fully stabilized or made meaningful progress in their treatment.

The complexity and challenges inherent in the forensic hospital system underscored the critical need for comprehensive mental health support services, as well as ongoing efforts to streamline processes and alleviate backlogs. Our work was not merely about restoring competency for legal proceedings but also about ensuring that individuals received the care and support necessary for their overall well-being and recovery.

I have significant concerns regarding the current approach to competency restoration. While it is true that defendants with mental illness can achieve competency to stand trial, it is important to recognize that this does not necessarily equate to complete remission of their illness. The reality is that even if someone is deemed competent, their mental health condition may still pose a significant risk of deterioration, especially if they are returned to a jail setting.

Jails are inherently dangerous environments for defendants with chronic mental illness awaiting trial. The stress, isolation, and lack of adequate mental health support can impair their condition and increase the likelihood of crisis or harm. However, it is also true that some defendants have committed serious crimes and pose a risk to public safety, necessitating some form of confinement pending trial.

In cases when an individual with mental illness does not understand the charges or the reason for their incarceration, it is essential that they undergo competency restoration. This is not only crucial for ensuring the fairness of the judicial system but also for safeguarding the rights and well-being of the defendant.

An analogy can be drawn to medical care. Just as it would be unethical to discharge a patient from the hospital with an untreated fracture, uncontrolled diabetes, or without proper rehabilitation following a stroke, it is similarly unjust to subject defendants with mental illness to legal proceedings without addressing their mental health needs.

Before individuals with mental illness are returned to the courtroom to face charges that could have lifelong consequences, they must be viewed through a lens of compassion and understanding. This means prioritizing their mental health needs and ensuring that they receive appropriate treatment and support to stabilize their condition.

Ultimately, the goal should be to provide comprehensive mental health care, addressing both the legal and therapeutic aspects of the defendant's situation. By recognizing the complexities of mental illness and the challenges it presents, we can work toward a more just and humane approach to competency restoration and criminal justice overall.

Regrettably, justice often remains elusive within a system that is overwhelmed by bureaucracy and is ill-equipped to handle the complexities of mental illness. Every day, persons with mental health conditions are returned to environments—jails and prisons—where they are meant to be rehabilitated and reintegrated into society, but instead find themselves further marginalized and dehumanized.

The truth is that jails and prisons, by their very design, are institutions that strip away dignity, erode self-worth, and perpetuate cycles of trauma. Rather than fostering rehabilitation and promoting mental well-being, these environments often exacerbate existing mental health issues and subject individuals to further harm.

The bureaucratic hurdles and systemic shortcomings only compound the challenges. Overwhelmed by caseloads and lacking the necessary resources, authorities may struggle to provide adequate mental health care and support, leaving many people to languish in conditions that are detrimental to their mental and physical health.

It is essential to recognize that the inherent purpose of jails and prisons is not to uplift or empower but rather to punish and control. The oppressive nature of these environments serves to reinforce power imbalances and perpetuate cycles of oppression, particularly for those already marginalized due to their mental health status.

To truly achieve justice in the mental health context, we must confront the underlying systemic issues and prioritize human rights and dignity. This requires comprehensive reforms aimed at diverting individuals away from incarceration and toward community-based mental health treatment and support services. Additionally, we must invest in alternative approaches to justice that prioritize rehabilitation, restoration, and healing rather than punishment and retribution.

100

Ultimately, the path to justice for those with mental illness demands a fundamental shift in our approach—one that acknowledges their inherent worth and dignity as human beings and works to create environments that nurture rather than impair their well-being. Anything less perpetuates injustice and the cycle of suffering for those most in need of compassion and support.

During my fifteen-year tenure within the Miami-Dade County jail system, the volume of cases was staggering—often reaching 100,000 bookings annually. Over the course of my career, this meant that I had the potential to encounter an astounding 1.5 million individuals. During this influx, a critical aspect of our protocol was the thorough screening process conducted for everyone who was arrested.

Led by a dedicated team comprising nurses, social workers, and psychiatrists, the screening process was initiated at the time of booking. This comprehensive assessment aimed to address both physical and mental health concerns, recognizing the intertwined nature of these issues.

Key questions were posed to gauge overall health status and to identify any underlying mental health conditions. Queries such as, "Have you ever consulted with a psychiatrist before?" and "Have you ever experienced thoughts of self-harm or suicide?" were pivotal in uncovering potential mental health needs.

By conducting these screenings on intake, we endeavored to identify those who might require immediate medical attention or mental health intervention. The goal was not only to address acute health concerns but also to initiate appropriate referrals for ongoing care and support throughout their time in custody.

This proactive approach to screening underscored our commitment to providing comprehensive care, recognizing the importance of early intervention in addressing mental health needs. Despite the overwhelming volume of individuals passing through our doors, each screening represented an opportunity to identify and support those in need, ultimately contributing to the broader goal of promoting health and well-being within the jail system.

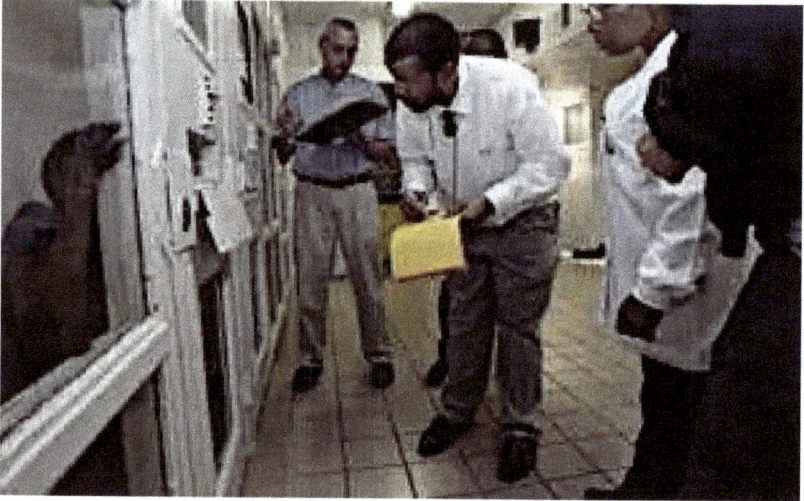

Dr. Joseph Poitier, Jr. and others pictured for "The Forgotten Floor" circa 2007

The Miami-Dade County jail operated on a meticulous classification system, considering various factors such as nature of charges, prior arrest history, and presence of any mental or physical impairments. However, when it came to prioritizing these classification criteria, the presence of mental illness took precedence above all else at the time of booking.

This prioritization stemmed from a fundamental principle: while jails are designed to confine individuals, they are not intended to endanger lives. According to our laws, we are entrusted with the responsibility of safeguarding the well-being and preserving the lives of those who are arrested, regardless of their circumstances.

The classification system within the Miami-Dade County jail consisted of several facilities, each serving specific purposes within the broader framework of the criminal justice system. These included:

- The Pretrial Detention Center: This facility, which has stood as long as I have, served as a crucial hub for defendants awaiting trial. Here, individuals were held during the pretrial phase, pending resolution of their legal proceedings. The staff at this facility played a pivotal role as gatekeepers for the intake process, serving as ground zero where the majority of inmates were booked.

- The Women's Annex: Providing specialized accommodations for female detainees, the Women's Annex ensured gender-specific care and support for women.

- The Stockade: The stockade played a vital role in housing individuals with specific classification needs or serving particular sentences.

- The Turner Guilford Knight Center: This facility, also known as the Turner Guilford Knight Corrections Center, served as a central location within the jail system, accommodating a diverse range of offenders and providing various support services. It also served as an entry way into the jail system or booking station similarly to the Pretrial Detention Center.

- The Metro West Detention System: Offering modern facilities and resources, the Metro West Detention System played a crucial role in meeting the evolving needs of the Miami-Dade County jail system. This jail housed most of the inmates in the jail system.

Each of these facilities played a unique role in the classification and management of criminal defendants. By prioritizing the identification and accommodation of those with mental illness, the Miami-Dade County jail system aimed to uphold its commitment to humane treatment and ensure the safety and well-being of all those in custody.

The Pretrial Detention Center, while serving a critical function, starkly revealed the shortcomings of older correctional facilities. Its aging infrastructure stood in contrast to modern facilities equipped with automated systems, relying instead on manual controls to manage access to its cells. This outdated approach not only highlighted inefficiencies but also raised concerns about security and inmate safety. In an era where advancements in technology have transformed various industries, the reliance on manual systems within older correctional facilities underscores the urgent need for infrastructure updates and modernization efforts.

This manual operation of cell doors represented a significant aspect of the facility's infrastructure, requiring staff members to physically engage with each door to open or close it as needed. This method of control, while functional, may have presented logistical challenges and required additional manpower to ensure smooth operations within the facility.

The age of the Pretrial Detention Center further reflected the challenges faced by staff and inmates alike. While efforts were likely made to maintain the facility and ensure its safety and functionality, the limitations imposed by its aging infrastructure may have posed ongoing concerns for those responsible for its operation and management.

Despite its antiquated features, the Pretrial Detention Center remained an essential component of the Miami-Dade County jail system, providing necessary accommodations for those awaiting trial. However, the manual control of cell doors served as a tangible reminder of the facility's dated design and the ongoing need for investment in modernizing correctional infrastructure to meet the evolving needs and standards of the criminal justice system.

During my nearly fifteen-year tenure in that system, I had the privilege of evaluating and treating thousands of inmates. This work was made possible through the dedicated efforts of a diverse team, including social workers, nurses, and correctional officers, who worked tirelessly alongside me, providing crucial support and assistance in delivering care to those in need.

Remarkably, many of the correctional officers I encountered had developed a deep sense of commitment and compassion toward the inmate population. Despite the inherent challenges of working within a jail environment, these officers demonstrated a genuine dedication to their roles, often serving on the ninth floor for several years across various shifts.

Shortly after I began working at the jail, I received a call from one of the officers after hours. I did not return his call that evening, and I met his wrath the following day. He towered over men in his green overalls. He was known as an expert with his hands and feet and was notorious throughout the jail and among the inmates. I will not say exactly what he told me, but to my surprise, he called me because he was concerned about the status of an inmate. I was dazed by his concern about the inmate's safety and mental well-being. He and I later became good friends. He gained a certain respect for me and I for him.

The attitude that this officer displayed was one that was characteristic of all the officers who worked on the ninth floor. They were there because they wanted to be there and wanted to help take care of these inmates with brain or mental disorders. I would review the latest findings with one officer in particular and we would discuss current trends and psychiatric problems found in the jails from time to time.

However, it has become increasingly evident in recent years that the demands of working in a jail environment can take a toll on the mental and emotional well-being of correctional officers. The nature of their work exposes them to high levels of stress and trauma on a daily basis, as they navigate potentially volatile situations and confront the realities of violence and aggression within the facility.

The impact of this exposure to trauma extends beyond the workplace, often spilling over into the personal lives of correctional officers. They may carry home their frustrations and anxieties, affecting their relationships with loved ones and their overall mental health.

Witnessing incidents of injury and violence or managing inmates in an agitated or psychotic state can be particularly distressing for correctional officers. The need to use restraints or administer involuntary medication adds another layer of complexity to their already demanding responsibilities, further contributing to their emotional burden.

As we reflect on the challenges faced by all individuals working in the criminal justice system, it is crucial to recognize and address the mental health needs of correctional officers. Providing adequate support, resources, and training can help mitigate the impact of trauma and stress, ensuring the well- being of those who play a vital role in maintaining safety and order within correctional facilities.

In the Miami-Dade County jail system, we adhered to stringent policies and protocols governing the use of involuntary medication and restraints, akin to those implemented in the Crisis Unit of Miami's prominent county hospital. These guidelines were designed to ensure the safety and well-being of both inmates and staff, while also upholding ethical standards of care.

Our health-care team operated under the umbrella of the Jackson Behavioral Health System, confirming our commitment to providing comprehensive mental health services within the correctional setting. Known as Corrections Health Services, our department played a pivotal role in addressing the unique health care needs of inmates, particularly those suffering with mental illness.

Under the oversight of an administrator who directly reported to one of the administrators at the main hospital campus, our team operated with a shared mission of delivering quality health care to all. This hierarchical structure ensured accountability and alignment with the broader goals and standards of the health-care system.

By integrating our health-care services with those of the larger hospital system, we were able to leverage resources, expertise, and best practices to optimize care delivery. This collaborative approach facilitated seamless coordination between correctional and community health-care services, enhancing continuity of care for individuals transitioning between incarceration and reintegration into society.

Our affiliation with the Jackson Behavioral Health System displayed our commitment to upholding the highest standards of professionalism, ethics, and patient-centered care. Despite the challenges inherent in providing health care within a correctional environment, our team remained steadfast in our dedication to promoting health, dignity, and well-being for everyone in our care.

On the Pretrial Detention Center's ninth floor, our facility was structured into three distinct units, each meticulously designed to cater to the diverse needs of mentally challenged inmates.

- Acute Unit: This unit served as a critical lifeline for those experiencing acute mental health crises, as well as those deemed at imminent risk of self-harm or suicide. Here, our dedicated staff provided round-the-clock monitoring, intensive therapeutic interventions, and stringent suicide precautions to ensure the safety and well-being of every inmate.

- B-Wing: Housing individuals with chronic mental illnesses, the B-Wing provided a supportive environment for those requiring ongoing management and treatment. While not in an acute state, these inmates faced challenges with medication compliance or other aspects of their mental health care, necessitating close monitoring and intervention to prevent relapse or deterioration.

- A-Wing: Functioning as a transitional space, the A-Wing accommodated inmates charged with non-serious offenses and those transitioning from acute or chronic care units. The primary objective of the mental health treatment team, which included both medical professionals and correctional officers, was to stabilize people sufficiently to facilitate their transition to a less restrictive environment on the eighth floor. Here, inmates could enjoy increased privileges, such as communal interaction and access to recreational facilities, while continuing to receive necessary mental health support.

Below the ninth floor, the Pretrial Detention Center comprised administrative and housing floors, each serving distinct purposes. The administrative seventh floor facilitated the smooth functioning of daily operations, while the lower floors—sixth, fifth, and fourth—housed inmates facing more serious charges and residing in harsher living conditions.

These lower floors were designated for individuals considered potentially dangerous, including those accused of serious crimes that had garnered media attention. Here, strict security measures were implemented to maintain order and ensure the

108

safety of all inmates and staff members. Separate cells were allocated for super-max predators and sexual predators, reflecting the facility's commitment to managing high-risk inmates while upholding the principles of safety and security.

In essence, the organizational structure of the Pretrial Detention Center exemplified a holistic approach to managing inmates with mental health needs within the confines of the criminal justice system. Through specialized units, tailored interventions, and a dedicated team of professionals, we aimed to promote rehabilitation, ensure safety, and uphold the dignity of everyone in our care.

Apart from the Pretrial Detention Center, which housed inmates with mental health needs in specialized units, there were three additional jails catering to the general population of male inmates: the Stockade, Metro West, and the Turner Guilford Knight Center.

These facilities primarily accommodated those who had not been diagnosed with a mental illness or, if diagnosed, were deemed capable of functioning within a standard cell environment. The inmates housed in these jails were typically able to manage their day-to-day activities without the specialized support and interventions required for those with acute mental health challenges.

Over the course of my fifteen-year tenure, I witnessed the ebb and flow of the jail population, which consistently hovered around 6,500 inmates. What struck me most during this time was the sheer number of inmates with mental health issues.

On any given day, approximately 1,000 inmates, representing nearly one third of the total population, were reliant on various medications to manage their mental health disorders. This was 1 out of every 6 individuals. This staggering statistic documented the pervasive nature of mental illness and the significant challenges it posed for inmates and correctional staff alike.

As I navigated my role within the facility, I couldn't help but reflect on the complex interplay between mental health and the criminal justice system. Each inmate represented a unique story, a convergence of personal struggles and societal factors that had led them to this point. And yet, amid the chaos and confinement, there existed a pressing need for compassionate care and support for each of them.

Despite the daunting numbers, I remained steadfast in my commitment to providing quality care and advocating for improved mental health services within the jail. It was a journey fraught with challenges, but one that was undeniably crucial in addressing the intersection of mental illness and incarceration in our community.

In my experience, people suffering from major mental illnesses often displayed symptoms consistent with their condition, even within the confines of a jail environment. Hallucinations, paranoia, and medication refusal were common indicators of acute mental illness, requiring careful observation and intervention by trained professionals.

Years of experience working with mentally ill inmates enabled our team to quickly distinguish between those experiencing genuine mental health crises and those exhibiting behavior unrelated to mental illness. This level of competency and confidence was cultivated through extensive training and hands-on experience, allowing us to effectively triage and prioritize care for inmates based on their specific needs.

In medical school I always wondered why we would review the same type of cases over and over and over again. It was to gain expertise and knowledge. It was so that we could diagnose different type of illnesses with our eyes closed. I often watch the video on YouTube in which Micheal Jordan

110

taunts Patrick Ewing and makes a free throw with his eyes closed.

My most terrifying but successful moment occurred during an elective rotation in urology my senior year. The surgical team I was assigned to was about to complete a procedure when it incidentally discovered a hernia. My attending asked me if I wanted to close the repair.

I had watched sutures being placed many times and read about the procedure in my surgery book, but to close a repair on a sedated human being was uncharted territory to me. I wanted to impress my attending. I did not want to be a failure. It took me nearly five minutes—while shaking, trembling, and sweating— but I was successful. My attending probably could have done it in seconds. That is why repetition is so key to learning and why my team members and I were so successful at rendering care to a very difficult population.

By leveraging our expertise and understanding of mental health dynamics, we were able to ensure that patients received appropriate care and support, regardless of the complexities of their condition or the challenges posed by the jail environment. This commitment to compassionate and competent care showed our dedication to promoting the health, safety, and dignity of all patients within our responsibility.

In jail environments, episodes of feigned or fabricated mental illness are not uncommon, often motivated by various secondary gains such as seeking safety or avoiding conflicts with other inmates. Prisoners may simulate symptoms of mental illness in an attempt to gain placement on the ninth floor, where they perceive a reduced risk of harm or coercion from fellow inmates. However, our team remained vigilant in identifying such cases and promptly subjected them to thorough evaluation and observation to discern the authenticity of their claims. Upon careful assessment, those found to be feigning mental illness were promptly returned to the general population, ensuring the integrity of our mental health services and maintaining the safety of all inmates.

The team I had the privilege of working with consistently showed total confidence in my abilities, and I reciprocated that trust by deeply respecting the invaluable roles played by every team member, including the correctional officers. Over time, our collaboration fostered a close-knit bond, and I became intimately familiar with each person on the ninth floor. This familiarity was a testament to our team's commitment to inmate care and to our shared dedication to ensuring the well-being of those under our charge.

Reflecting on my tenure at the jail, I have few regrets about the decisions made or the quality of care provided to inmates. Despite the formidable challenges posed by the high-acuity cases we encountered, we managed to keep the number of deaths remarkably low—fewer than ten over the span of fifteen years. This remarkable achievement stands as a confirmation of the dedication and diligence of our team.

Our daily routine involved conducting rounds on the ninth floor, diligently ensuring that each inmate received the necessary care and attention. The flow of inmates through the jail system followed a structured process—from inception at booking, to specialized care on the ninth floor, to transition to the eighth floor—before finally moving on to general population and ultimately to the stockade, Metro West, or Turner Guilford Knight Correctional Center (TGK). This systematic approach allowed us to effectively manage the influx of inmates while prioritizing their well-being.

It's worth noting that the length of stay on each floor varied based on the severity of the inmates' needs. Some required extended care, necessitating longer stays on specific floors to ensure that their health and safety were adequately addressed. This flexibility further demonstrated our commitment to

112

providing individualized care tailored to the special circumstances of each inmate.

There were two incidents which trouble me to this day. One was that of a young man who hung himself in the acute area of the ninth floor. He was housed in the acute area but was not placed in a Ferguson garment, which was a meshed gown placed on acutely suicidal inmates.

He hung himself by fashioning a piece of a sheet that he tore up and used as a noose. I was not there that late evening, but everything that could go wrong did go wrong. He was less than four feet from the nurses' station and within steps of officers. He happened to be placed in a cell with a deaf mute. Later it was learned that his cellmate tried to alert staff but could not because he was mute.

After this young man's death, which was traumatizing for me, I would actually assign inmates specific cells and on occasion have an officer sit directly in front of a cell.

One high profile inmate stayed on the ninth floor with an officer in the front of his cell during his entire period of incarceration. I wanted to do my best to ensure that no one else died under my supervision, either direct or indirectly.

We had one more near death which also troubles me to this day. Again, it was a bad outcome in a bad environment. Someone jumped from a top bunk. He did not die, but he came close.

When the cameras came to the ninth floor and shot footage of two, three, or sometimes four inmates in a cell, I cringed with anxiety. However, I did not want anyone else to die under my watch. If forced to choose the lesser of two evils, I would rather they be crammed in a cell than hanging from the end of a noose.

While mental illness can indeed be feigned, it is essential to recognize that genuine cases of mental illness are complex and multifaceted, requiring skilled assessment and intervention. As professionals, we were trained to distinguish between authentic mental health challenges and deceptive behavior, ensuring that inmates received appropriate care and support based on their true needs.

During my entire career, I can only remember once having to retract my decision-making processes, which often included participation from others, but in one case a final decision was left to me alone. I kept an inmate in the acute care area for several months because he would not talk. I would walk by his cell almost every day but he remained mute. I thought that I would observe something that would give me a greater clue as to what was going on with him, but I never did until two well-dressed men with ties and badges walked onto the floor.

They asked me what I knew about the inmate. I said "not much" because he had not been talking. The officers later informed me that he had been involved in a murder. I remember having to testify under oath that I had been wrong in my assessment of this inmate insinuating that I had misdiagnosed this young man. It was later revealed that not only could this inmate talk, but he did also not in fact have a mental disorder.

Of the thousands of inmates I saw during my fifteen-year career, his story was the only one for which I had to say that I made the wrong assessment, mainly due to not thoroughly reviewing every detail in a patient's file. Before that incident, I had made a point of not reading the full details of every inmate's arrest from the stance of ensuring I evaluated every individual on a case-by-case basis and not prejudging their treatment plan based on their charges. This approach was intended to free me of prejudice or preconceived notions. However, this young man made me change that practice. In all high-profile cases of individuals housed on the ninth floor, I

114

now made it a point to review their arrest affidavits in careful detail.

Reflecting on my education and training, I recall a fundamental principle instilled in me during my undergraduate studies: the concept that mathematics is the only exact science. This axiom resonated deeply with me, highlighting the universal and immutable nature of mathematical principles. Unlike other disciplines, where variables and interpretations may vary, mathematics offers a singular, indisputable truth—a concept that transcends geographical, linguistic, and cultural boundaries.

While the human body may exhibit anatomical variations and complexities, mathematics remains a steadfast and universal language, offering clarity and precision in its principles. In the realm of medical science, this adherence to rigor and objectivity is paramount, guiding our approach to diagnosis, treatment, and research. It underscores the importance of evidence-based practice and the pursuit of knowledge grounded in empirical observation and mathematical certainty.

Indeed, while the study of medicine may involve inherent uncertainties and complexities, the guiding principles of mathematics serve as beacons of clarity and certainty, anchoring our understanding and practice in a realm of immutable truth.

Chapter 10: Navigating Quasi Freedom for the Mentally Ill

As a Black doctor deeply immersed in the realm of mental health care within the criminal justice system, I have witnessed firsthand the complex interplay between freedom and confinement for individuals grappling with mental illness. Within this intricate landscape, several key themes emerge, each demanding careful consideration and advocacy for equitable and compassionate care.

The Paradox of Freedom
In many ways, the concept of quasi freedom for the mentally ill embodies a paradoxical reality. While individuals may be granted certain liberties, they remain tethered to a system marked by surveillance, control, and stigma. I am acutely aware of the disproportionate impact of these dynamics on marginalized communities, where systemic inequities intersect with mental health vulnerabilities.

Balancing the inherent tension between autonomy and safety requires a nuanced understanding of cultural, socioeconomic, and historical factors that shape experiences of mental illness and incarceration.

Transitional Care
Transitioning from incarceration to community-based care settings presents formidable challenges, particularly for Black communities disproportionately affected by the criminal justice system. Structural barriers, including limited access to mental health services, housing instability, and discrimination, exacerbate the difficulties of reintegration. I have always been an advocate for comprehensive, culturally competent transitional support programs that address the unique needs and experiences of Black communities. This includes expanding access to mental health resources, promoting housing stability, and fostering supportive networks to

mitigate the risk of recidivism and promote long-term recovery.

Legal and Ethical Considerations
Within the framework of quasi freedom, navigating the legal and ethical dimensions of mental health care requires a deep commitment to justice, fairness, and human rights. As a Black doctor, I confront the legacy of structural racism and systemic oppression that permeates the criminal justice system, shaping policies and practices that disproportionately impact Black people. From informed consent to involuntary treatment, I advocate for policies and practices that prioritize autonomy, dignity, and cultural humility. Drawing on principles of social justice and antiracism, I challenge discriminatory practices and work toward equitable mental health care systems that uphold the rights and dignity of all, regardless of race or ethnicity.

Collaborative Solutions
Addressing the complex needs of those transitioning from incarceration to the community demands a collaborative and multidisciplinary approach. I recognize the importance of community partnerships, peer support networks, and culturally responsive services in promoting healing and resilience. By fostering collaboration among mental health providers, community organizations, and criminal justice stakeholders, we can develop holistic and sustainable solutions that address the underlying social determinants of mental illness and incarceration within Black communities.

Advocacy and Empowerment
Central to the pursuit of equitable mental health care is the amplification of marginalized voices and the empowerment of individuals with lived experience of mental illness. I stand in complete solidarity with Black activists, advocates, and community leaders fighting against systemic oppression and advocating for transformative change. By centering the voices

118

and experiences of Black people, we can challenge stigma, dismantle structural barriers, and foster a culture of inclusion, equity, and belonging within mental health care systems.

Navigating quasi freedom for the mentally ill requires a deep commitment to justice, equity, and compassion. I am committed to challenging systemic injustices, amplifying marginalized voices, and advocating for policies and practices that prioritize the rights and dignity of all, particularly those impacted by the intersecting forces of racism, poverty, and mental illness. Through collective action and solidarity, we can strive toward a future where mental health care is truly equitable, accessible, and inclusive for all.

Tragic Losses Spark Heightened Awareness and Action

The tragic reality of untreated severe mental illness has left law enforcement officers (LEOs) grappling with increasingly dangerous situations and has catalyzed the development of mental health diversion initiatives. Too often, people with severe mental illness are abandoned by the mental health system, leading to potentially disastrous outcomes when they pose a threat to themselves or others. This not only endangers the individuals themselves but also puts LEOs at risk when they are forced to intervene in volatile situations.

Many of these tragic incidents could have been prevented if Assisted Outpatient Treatment (AOT) laws were in place. AOT laws provide mechanisms to return the care of the most severely mentally ill back to the mental health system. By allowing courts to order offenders with a history of severe mental illness and violence to accept treatment as a condition of living in the community, AOT laws ensure that those in need receive the care and support necessary to prevent crises.

Research has shown a correlation between homicides and civil commitment statutes, with fewer homicides occurring in jurisdictions where dangerousness is not required for commitment. AOT laws have been proven to dramatically reduce arrest rates, incarceration, homelessness, and suicide among individuals with severe mental illness, thereby alleviating the burden on law enforcement resources.

Incidents of LEOs being harmed or killed by people with untreated severe mental illness underscore the urgent need for proactive measures such as AOT laws. These statistics are not intended to demonize individuals with mental illness but to emphasize the critical importance of implementing legislation that prioritizes public safety while also addressing the needs of those struggling with severe mental health issues.

Legislation such as Laura's Law in California and Kendra's Law in New York serve as models for AOT laws that have been endorsed by organizations advocating for people with mental illness (such as National Alliance on Mental Illness (NAMI)) and those advocating for public safety such as the National Sheriffs' Association. By working together toward a common goal of implementing AOT laws, we can create safer communities, protect LEOs, and save taxpayer money while ensuring that those with severe mental illness receive the care and support they desperately need.

From the sorrowful loss of numerous law enforcement officers worldwide, a profound revelation emerged: the pressing necessity for a transformative approach to addressing mental health crises inside the criminal justice system. These heartbreaking incidents highlighted the critical juncture between mental illness and law enforcement, shedding light on the inherent risks and intricate challenges faced by both individuals in distress and the officers entrusted with their care.

In the aftermath of these tragedies, stakeholders from law enforcement agencies, mental health advocacy groups, and community organizations united to redefine how society confronts mental health emergencies. Acknowledging that conventional law enforcement responses often escalate tensions and heighten the potential for violence, a new paradigm began to take shape: mental health diversion.

At its essence, mental health diversion aims to redirect people in crisis away from the criminal justice system and toward appropriate mental health services and resources. Instead of resorting solely to punitive measures like arrest and incarceration, this approach prioritizes early intervention, crisis de-escalation, and access to comprehensive mental health treatment and support services.

Key components of mental health diversion initiatives include:

Intervention Teams (CIT)
These are specialized law enforcement units trained to respond to mental health crises with compassion, de-escalation techniques, and connections to community-based mental health resources. CIT programs equip officers with the skills and knowledge needed to recognize signs of mental illness, communicate effectively with individuals in crisis, and facilitate access to appropriate care.

Mobile Crisis Response Teams
These are multidisciplinary teams comprising mental health professionals, social workers, and peer support specialists who provide on-site crisis intervention and support to people experiencing mental health crises. These teams offer immediate assistance, assessment, and linkage to community-based services, reducing the need for law enforcement involvement.

Prebooking Diversion Programs
These options constitute collaborative efforts among law enforcement agencies, mental health providers, and judicial stakeholders to divert individuals with mental illness away

from the criminal justice system at the point of arrest. These programs offer alternatives to traditional prosecution, such as diversion to mental health treatment programs, supportive housing, or crisis stabilization centers.

Mental Health Courts

These are specialized court programs designed to address the unique needs of individuals with mental illness who come into contact with the criminal justice system. Mental health courts prioritize treatment over punishment, offering participants access to mental health treatment, substance abuse counseling, housing assistance, and other supportive services as an alternative to incarceration.

Community-Based Support Services

These services include robust community-based mental health supports, including crisis hotlines, outpatient counseling, psychiatric care, supportive housing, and peer support programs. They play a crucial role in preventing crises, promoting recovery, and supporting individuals with mental illness in their journey toward stability and wellness.

Unlike solutions conceived by academic elites, this strategy emerged from the collective determination of a community to address the challenges posed by mental illness. Alongside this grassroots effort, mental health diversion courts were established with the aim of redirecting individuals facing non-serious charges away from incarceration and toward comprehensive treatment in a hospital-like setting.

In South Florida, particularly in Miami-Dade County, Judge Steven Leifman has been a notable contributor to mental health advocacy, playing a significant role in initiating reforms of the region's criminal justice system. While his efforts have been impactful, it's important to note that the system remains flawed and in need of further improvement.

Judge Leifman's commitment to reform has made a lasting impression, both locally and nationally. Collaborative efforts under his guidance have brought together stakeholders such as law enforcement agencies, mental health providers, advocacy organizations, and community leaders to address mental health crises comprehensively and compassionately.

Through innovative initiatives, Judge Leifman has facilitated the creation of specialized mental health diversion programs and courts aimed at offering access to appropriate treatment and support services instead of incarceration. These programs seek to tackle the root causes of involvement in the criminal justice system while mitigating the risks associated with untreated mental illness.

It's essential to acknowledge that Judge Leifman has not been alone in these efforts. Other dedicated individuals and experts joined in a collective effort and contributed to the solutions. In 2007, alongside the late Michele Gillen, an esteemed investigative reporter, Judge Leifman conducted a tour of the ninth floor, revealing the deplorable conditions through Gillen's reporting, which exposed the ongoing challenges that still persist despite the judge's efforts. It was the first of multiple visits CBS4 Chief Investigative Reporter Michele Gillen made to the 9th floor of the Miami-Dade Pre-Trial Detention Center that captured the shocking conditions and treatment afforded the most vulnerable of mentally ill inmates.

Interviews were consistently plagued with a common denominator, there was little positivity to be found in discussions about the environment. Our team worked tirelessly to navigate the challenges we faced, but there was no denying the severity of the circumstances or to dress up the conditions in place. We operated under duress as a daily mode of operation, often enduring conditions comparable to those experienced by the inmates themselves.

There were days when the air conditioning failed, leaving us to contend with stifling heat and overwhelming odors. We witnessed the distressing sight of feces being thrown on cell windows, a harrowing reminder of the dehumanizing conditions faced by those in our care.

In the direst moments, we were called on to respond to life-threatening situations, such as resuscitating an inmate who had attempted to take his own life by hanging. These experiences reflected the gravity of the challenges we confronted daily and reinforced the urgent need for change.

These are indeed some of the horrific realities that medical and correctional staff faced, and I empathize deeply with the challenges they endured. For fifteen years, we labored tirelessly without acknowledgment, media attention, or awards.

It's crucial to emphasize that we, as caretakers, were not the perpetrators. Our role was to provide care and support to individuals within the justice system, often before they had their day in court. In a society prone to premature condemnation, we remained steadfast in our commitment to treating each individual with dignity and humanity.

Nearly every member of the medical and correctional staff who worked on the ninth floor did so with pride, dignity, and professionalism. They were some of the most dedicated colleagues I've ever had the privilege to work alongside.

Sadly, the issues within the jail system persisted even after my departure, and the eventual closure of the ninth floor in 2014 did little to address the systemic challenges. Randy Heath's tragic death in the summer of 2021 brought the Miami-Dade County jail back into the spotlight, shedding light on the ongoing struggles faced by inmates with severe psychiatric illnesses.

The details surrounding Heath's death are distressing, highlighting systemic failures in the provision of medical care within correctional facilities. His case serves as a vivid reminder of the urgent need for reform.

From left: Arleen Poitier; Michele Gillen; and Dr. Joseph Poitier, Jr.

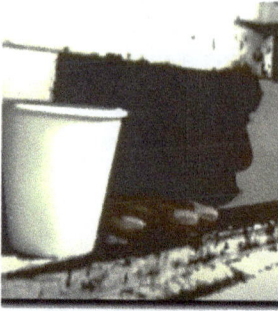

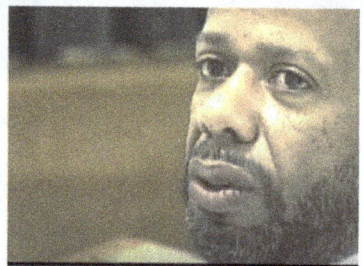

"The Forgotten Floor" Investigative Story by Michele Gillen from CBS
Chennel 4 in Miami, Florida found on https://www.cbsnews.com/miami/
from 2007

Miami-Dade Pre-Trial Detention Center circa 2007

From left: Judge Steven Leifman and Dr. Joseph Poitier Jr.

As of 2024, the legal proceedings surrounding Heath's death are ongoing, underscoring the complex and protracted nature of seeking justice in cases of institutional negligence. It is my hope that his case will serve as a catalyst for meaningful change and a renewed commitment to ensuring the well-being and dignity of all within our justice system.

Through Judge Leifman's advocacy and collaborative efforts, Miami-Dade County has become a model for innovative approaches to the crisis. His work has not only improved outcomes but also has enhanced public safety and reduced the burden on law enforcement resources. As a result, Judge Leifman's influence extends far beyond the boundaries of Miami-Dade County, serving as inspiration for similar initiatives across the nation.

Initially, the concept of mental health and problem-solving courts was met with trepidation, caution, and resistance from institutions outside the jail environment. However, as communities confronted the increasingly complex intersection of mental health and criminal justice, the need for innovative approaches became undeniable.

Despite the initial hesitancy, the evolution of diversion initiatives stands as an example of the power of community-driven solutions and the potential for transformative change. By prioritizing early intervention, access to treatment, and collaborative partnerships between law enforcement and mental health professionals, communities have endeavored to prevent tragedies while safeguarding the well-being of people in crisis.

The gradual acceptance and adoption of diversion programs reflect a shift in societal attitudes toward mental illness and criminal justice reform. Through concerted efforts to address the root causes of mental health crises and to provide comprehensive support services, communities have sought to break the cycle of incarceration and improve outcomes.

128

As diversion initiatives continue to evolve and expand, they offer hope for a more compassionate, effective, and equitable response to mental health challenges. By embracing community-driven solutions and fostering collaboration across sectors, communities can strive toward a future where individuals in crisis receive the care and support they need to thrive, rather than facing incarceration and further harm.

Chapter 11: Amplifying Voices: Advocating for the Underrepresented

As a Black male doctor, navigating professional spaces often means confronting systemic biases and advocating for the underrepresented. In this chapter, I delve into the importance of amplifying voices that have historically been marginalized and overlooked. From challenging the status quo in medical settings to advocating for equitable access to health care for underserved communities, I share insights and experiences that highlight the power of speaking up for those who have been silenced. Join me as we explore the journey of advocacy and the transformative impact it can have on creating a more inclusive and just society.

Being intimately involved in the early stages of meetings with community stakeholders, jail officials, and courtroom authorities, I can attest that advocating for the diversion strategy was challenging. Surprisingly, some of the most resistant parties were my own colleagues, fellow psychiatrists, who appeared unwilling to extend their care to mentally ill inmates housed in the Miami-Dade County jail system.

I found myself grappling with a perplexing question: why should an individual's location, particularly if they are incarcerated, dictate the level of care they receive? It became evident that this reluctance stemmed from a pervasive stigma surrounding mental illness, coupled with misconceptions about the behaviors associated with it. Nuisance behaviors such as public urination, disturbances, and noncompliance with medication often led to individuals being unfairly blamed for their predicament.

As a Black male doctor, I was acutely aware of the intersectionality of race and mental health stigma, which compounded the challenges faced by incarcerated individuals

131

seeking proper care. This experience highlighted the urgent need to confront systemic biases within the medical community and advocate for equitable treatment for all, regardless of their circumstances.

It was disheartening to witness the reluctance of some psychiatric colleagues to continue providing care to patients they had previously treated in the general community simply because they were now incarcerated. This disparity in treatment only served to further marginalize and stigmatize individuals with mental illness, perpetuating a cycle of neglect and inadequate care. As a Black psychiatrist who has primarily cared for Black people, this reality deeply affected me and lingered in my conscience.

The absence of Black community members during the initial stakeholder meetings, which were pivotal in the process, was concerning. This lack of representation underscores systemic issues of exclusion and marginalization, particularly in the crucial aspect of diverting mentally ill individuals from the jail system. Diversion programs aim to offer alternative pathways for individuals struggling with mental health challenges, steering them away from incarceration and toward appropriate mental health treatment and support services. The absence of Black voices in these discussions not only highlights disparities in access to mental health resources but also raises questions about the equity and effectiveness of diversion initiatives. It serves as a poignant reminder of the ongoing work needed to prioritize diversion efforts and ensure that they are inclusive, responsive, and equitable for all members of the community.

Despite the initial challenges and skepticism, the diversion strategy gradually gained momentum and evolved into a national phenomenon. We began by diverting offenders with low-level misdemeanors and eventually individuals with third-degree felony charges, identifying them as mentally ill, and providing treatment in a hospital-like setting. They would then

132

be stabilized and released into the community with the necessary support, including housing and follow-up care. In some cases, successful compliance with treatment meant that their charges would never be recorded as misdemeanors or felonies, offering them a chance to rebuild their lives without the burden of a criminal record.

My tenure in the jail system would not have been possible without the support and admiration of the dedicated staff who worked alongside me. While it is impossible to name everyone who contributed to our efforts, I must acknowledge Theodore Thomas, a senior social worker whose expertise and commitment were invaluable. Theodore transitioned from New Horizons Community Mental Health Center, one of the pioneering institutions in Florida providing outpatient care. His presence and expertise were instrumental in navigating the complexities of caring for our jail population.

Theodore's transition from New Horizons to the county system brought greater opportunities for him, but more important, it brought his compassionate care to a group often neglected by society—the lower socioeconomic class in Miami-Dade County. This population encompassed not only Black individuals but also other minorities such as Hispanics and those from other countries who were unfamiliar with the laws and systems of the United States. Despite the diverse backgrounds and challenges faced by these groups, his dedication and expertise made a profound impact on their lives.

Through his tireless efforts, many who left the jail were able to regain stability and maintain their mental well-being. Theodore's work exemplified the importance of compassionate and culturally competent care in addressing the needs of marginalized communities, leaving a lasting legacy of compassion and service.

Theodore's impact extended beyond his direct care for the inmates; he played a pivotal role in diversifying the staff in the jail. His ability to recruit other minority staff members proved his leadership and influence. Moreover, his demeanor was exceptionally well-suited for the challenging dynamics of a jail setting. He exuded a unique blend of pleasantness, wit, street smarts, and non-confrontational approach, which set the tone for the entire team.

The staff he recruited mirrored his demeanor, creating a cohesive and supportive work environment. One notable example is Allan Monica, LCSW, Esq., who started as a social worker and eventually became an attorney during his tenure at the jail. Allan remains a close friend to this day, a result of the lasting bonds forged in the intensity of his work environment.

It was here that I also cultivated some of my closest friendships, including Carter Wiggins, whom I had the privilege of mentoring. Carter has since made significant contributions to our community, providing care and support to those in the grip of various behavioral disorders I met my future fraternity brother Dr. Gibson Aristide during this period as well. The enduring camaraderie among Theodore, Allan, Carter, Gibson and myself reflects the tight connections formed through shared experiences and a shared commitment to serving others.

Among the vast array of experiences in psychiatric employment in a correctional setting, one story stands out vividly in my memory—a poignant narrative that exposes the tragic consequences of untreated mental illness colliding with the harsh realities of the criminal justice system.

The narrative begins with the distraught wife of an individual deeply suffering from untreated mental illness. Witnessing my discourse on the challenging conditions in Miami's jails, she reached out to me, her desperation palpable as she sought assistance for her husband, who exhibited early signs of

134

paranoid schizophrenia. Understanding the gravity of his situation, she implored me to intervene, recognizing the urgent need for professional help to avert a potential crisis.

From left: Dr. Joseph Poitier Jr. and Theodore Thomas

From left: Dr. Joseph Poitier Jr. and Carter Wiggins

When I met her husband, it was glaringly apparent that his condition presented formidable obstacles. Like many with schizophrenia, he had difficulty adhering to the prescribed treatment, rendering it arduous to effectively manage his symptoms. Despite our concerted efforts to offer guidance and support, his mental health deteriorated, eventually plummeting into a full-blown crisis.

In a chilling turn of events, in the throes of his mental turmoil he became embroiled in a harrowing high-speed chase with a Florida Highway Patrol officer. Tragically, the pursuit culminated in a devastating outcome, with the officer losing control of his vehicle and suffering grievous injuries. Subsequently, my patient was apprehended by other law enforcement officers, heralding a cascade of legal ramifications and an extended period of probation.

This distressing tale serves as a stark example of the profound challenges faced by people trapped in the unforgiving confines of the criminal justice system. It confirms the critical importance of comprehensive mental health support and intervention, particularly for those teetering on the brink of crisis, underscoring the urgent need for systemic reform to ensure that no one slips through the cracks of a flawed and strained system.

The officer involved in the chase demonstrated remarkable compassion by advocating for leniency in sentencing, a gesture that, in some measure, was granted by the presiding judge. This act of empathy proved pivotal, offering a glimmer of hope amid the darkness of the patient's circumstances.

Fortuitously, the patient emerged relatively unscathed from the legal ordeal, spared from prolonged incarceration or confinement. This favorable outcome can be attributed, in part, to his consistent compliance with medication and regular monitoring, facilitated by the supportive network that rallied around him. As a result, he has now been liberated from the constraints of court oversight, marking a triumphant milestone in his journey toward recovery.

This memory evokes the profound words of civil rights activist Rev. Dr. Martin Luther King Jr., who famously stated, "Our lives begin to end the day we become silent about things that matter." These words resonate deeply with me, serving as a powerful reminder of the imperative to speak out against injustice and champion causes of significance. Just as Dr. King emphasized the necessity of raising our voices in the face of oppression, so too must we advocate for the marginalized and underserved, particularly within the spheres of mental health and the criminal justice system.

As the ones who have the most influence and the capacity for impactful change, it is our responsibility to use our voices and resources to address systemic inequalities and ensure equitable access to care and justice for all. This commitment to advocacy and social justice lies at the heart of our collective duty to create a more just and compassionate society.

Judge Leifman's initial focus on the conditions of the jail's ninth floor was unprecedented for a sitting judge. He wasted no time in shining a spotlight on the dire situation, bringing cameras in to expose the appalling conditions that had long been hidden from public view. As the cameras captured the grim reality of the ninth floor, I found myself facing a moral dilemma. Despite the risk of repercussions, I felt compelled to speak out against the injustice unfolding before me. The thought of remaining silent in the face of such suffering was inconceivable, as it would have implied complicity with an environment that was fundamentally flawed and inhumane.

Despite my initial apprehension, I knew that remaining silent was not an option. It was a pivotal moment that reaffirmed my commitment to advocating for change and standing up against injustice. Expressing my views on camera was a decision rooted in my belief that every individual deserves to be treated with dignity and respect, especially those who are most vulnerable.

To my relief, I faced no reprimand from my administrators for speaking out. In fact, some even commended me for shedding light on the dire conditions of the ninth floor. This positive response validated my decision to raise my voice and served as a reminder that advocating for change is both necessary and impactful.

Moreover, I was heartened to see the dedication and compassion displayed by many of the officers who worked on the ninth and eighth floors. Their commitment to caring for inmates, even in the face of challenging circumstances, was a confirmation of their empathy and professionalism. Many of these officers had spent years in this environment, forging bonds with inmates and offering support and guidance whenever possible. Their actions exemplified the importance of empathy and human connection in fostering a more compassionate and just society.

Ultimately, it was through collaboration and mutual respect among officers, health-care professionals, and other stakeholders that we were able to effect meaningful reforms and create a more compassionate and effective system of care for those in need.

In the intricate web of our society's response to chronic mental illness, there's a collective responsibility that we must acknowledge. Instead of offering organized and potentially costly care, we often funnel suffering people into a prison system ill-equipped to address their complex needs. The ultimate price paid in this flawed system is sometimes nothing short of the loss of human life.

This systemic failure to provide adequate care for those with chronic mental illness reflects a broader societal neglect. It is a failure that implicates groups at every level of society, from policymakers and health-care providers to law enforcement and community members. Each of us, in our own way, contributes to this fractured system, whether through indifference, lack of awareness, or failure to advocate for change.

Yet, amid this acknowledgment of collective responsibility, there's also an opportunity for collective action. By recognizing the shortcomings of our current approach and committing to meaningful reform, we can begin to dismantle the barriers that block access to care and support.

Chapter 12: Changing of the Guards

"For evil to flourish, it is only necessary for good people to remain silent."

Martin Luther King Jr.

"The Noble King" by Deanna Pierce, 2024

In the realm of mental health inside correctional facilities, silence in the face of deplorable conditions not only perpetuates suffering but also allows injustice to thrive. In this chapter, we look into the imperative of breaking this silence and advocating for meaningful change.

The circumstances surrounding my departure from the Miami-Dade County jail coincided with a significant downturn in the stock market during the 2000s, amplifying the challenges already faced within the criminal justice system. The economic downturn strained budgets and resources, exacerbating existing inequities within our jail and prison systems. As financial pressures intensified, authorities grappled with difficult decisions regarding funding allocations, often resulting in reduced support for critical rehabilitation and reintegration programs for incarcerated individuals. Consequently, marginalized communities, disproportionately affected by poverty and systemic injustices, bore the brunt of these cutbacks, further widening the gap in access to essential services and opportunities for rehabilitation. Thus, amidst economic turmoil, the disparities and injustices entrenched within our correctional facilities became even more pronounced, underscoring the urgent need for comprehensive reform and investment in alternatives to incarceration.

The emergence of for-profit prisons brings to mind haunting reminders of a dark and troubling legacy in American history: slavery. Just as the institution of slavery commodified human lives for economic gain, for-profit prisons similarly prioritize profit over the well-being and rehabilitation of inmates. This parallel illuminates the deeply ingrained systemic injustices that persist within the criminal justice system.

Like the dehumanizing conditions endured by enslaved individuals, for-profit prisons subject inmates, including those with mental illness, to inhumane treatment and neglect in pursuit of financial profit. The profit-driven model incentivizes higher incarceration rates, longer sentences, and inadequate care, perpetuating a cycle of exploitation and disenfranchisement reminiscent of the era of slavery.

Prisons often face conflicts of interest due to their dual roles as facilities for incarceration and as providers of rehabilitation and support services. Some of the more notable common conflicts of interest within prison systems include:

- Privately operated prisons often prioritize profit over inmate rehabilitation, potentially influencing decisions on inmate care, length of stay, and staffing levels.

- Prison administrations may prioritize security and control over inmate welfare, leading to conflicts in implementing rehabilitative programs or addressing mental health issues.

- Conflicts can arise when prison staff are inadequately trained or have conflicting roles (e.g., limited staffing resources where security officers also responsible for mental health assessments).

- Conflicts may arise when prisons enter into contracts with external vendors (e.g., healthcare providers or food services) that prioritize cost-efficiency over quality of services.

- Political pressures or lobbying from stakeholders (e.g., private prison operators or unions) can influence policy decisions and funding allocations, potentially compromising inmate welfare.

- Conflicts may arise when prisons are tasked with enforcing legal standards while simultaneously facing challenges in meeting basic human rights and rehabilitative needs of inmates.

Keep in mind that for-profit prisons operate under a profit-driven model where financial incentives are tied to inmate occupancy rates. This creates a controversial dynamic where there's a potential incentive to lobby for stricter sentencing laws and harsher penalties, aiming to increase inmate populations and maximize revenue. Contracts between private prisons and government agencies often include occupancy guarantees, obligating a certain number of beds to be filled regardless of crime rates or public safety needs. In their quest to reduce costs and maximize profits, private prisons may cut corners on staffing, training, and inmate services, leading to concerns about lower wages, high turnover, and limited access to rehabilitative programs.

Transparency issues are a major consideration as well. Private prisons are not always subject to the same level of scrutiny as public institutions, making it challenging to assess conditions and treatment of inmates consistently and uniformly. Ongoing legal and ethical concerns persist, including allegations of inmate mistreatment, inadequate healthcare, and violations of constitutional rights. While proponents argue for cost savings and efficiency, critics highlight risks to inmate well-being and the integrity of the criminal justice system when profit motives influence incarceration practices.

Moreover, the disproportionate impact of for-profit prisons on marginalized communities, particularly Black and Brown, echoes the historical legacy of racial oppression and inequality. Just as slavery disproportionately affected Black Americans, the mass incarceration facilitated by for-profit prisons disproportionately targets and marginalizes communities of color, perpetuating systemic racism and social injustice.

By recognizing the parallels between for-profit prisons and the legacy of slavery, we can confront the systemic injustices and advocate for transformative reforms that prioritize human dignity, rehabilitation, and equitable treatment for all, regardless of race or socioeconomic status.

Profiting from the incarceration of individuals with mental illness represents a fundamental injustice that compromises the principles of freedom, rehabilitation, and human dignity. Rather than prioritizing financial gain, our focus should be on ensuring the well-being and successful reintegration of offenders into society.

Privatizing the incarceration process not only incentivizes higher incarceration rates but also fails to address the root causes of criminal behavior, including mental illness. By placing profit motives above the needs of incarcerated individuals, such a system perpetuates a cycle of exploitation and neglect, exacerbating the challenges faced by those struggling with mental health issues.

Instead of privatizing incarceration, we should direct our efforts toward privatizing essential support services aimed at facilitating successful reentry into society. This includes investing in job training programs, mental health treatment, housing assistance, and educational opportunities.

By prioritizing these support services, we can empower inmates with the tools and resources they need to rebuild their lives and contribute positively to their communities. This approach not only promotes rehabilitation and reduces recidivism but also upholds the principles of justice, fairness, and human dignity for all, including those with mental illness.

Key areas such as aftercare systems, job training programs, housing assistance, and educational initiatives play pivotal roles in facilitating successful reintegration into society. The importance of comprehensive follow-up support for those released from prison cannot be overstated, confirming the significance of reentry programs.

Reentry programs are designed to address the many challenges offenders encounter upon reentering their communities, including securing gainful employment, finding stable housing, accessing essential health-care services, and navigating social support systems. By providing targeted support in these areas, reentry programs aim to empower individuals to overcome barriers to successful reintegration and lead fulfilling, productive lives.

Reentry programs recognize the interconnected nature of these challenges and adopt a holistic approach to support. By addressing not only immediate needs such as housing and employment but also long-term goals such as education and skill-building, these programs equip people with the tools and resources necessary to thrive post-incarceration.

Ultimately, investing in comprehensive reentry programs is essential for breaking the cycle of incarceration and promoting positive outcomes. By providing tailored support and opportunities for growth and development, these programs contribute to a more just and equitable society where all have the opportunity to rebuild their lives and realize their full potential.

Many people, such as Kenneth Chenault, the former CEO of American Express, recognize the value and significance of reentry programs. Their commitment to supporting initiatives aimed at reintegrating individuals leaving prisons and jails underscores the importance of investing in comprehensive reentry services.

Through generous contributions like Mr. and Mrs. Chenault's one-million-dollar donation, these initiatives receive vital financial support for programs that address the diverse needs of formerly incarcerated individuals. By funding job training programs, housing assistance, educational initiatives, and other essential services, these donations enable reentry programs to empower them with the resources and support necessary for successful reintegration into society.

Jeff Bezos, the billionaire philanthropist and founder of Amazon, has also recognized the critical need for reform of the criminal justice system. In a groundbreaking move, Bezos allocated one-hundred-million dollars to attorney and activist Van Jones to spearhead the development of innovative programs aimed at tackling two pressing issues: reducing incarceration rates and generating job opportunities for the formerly incarcerated.

This substantial investment reflects Bezos's commitment to addressing the systemic challenges that perpetuate cycles of incarceration and hinder successful reintegration into society. By entrusting Van Jones with the significant funding, Bezos acknowledges the expertise and dedication of those working on the front lines of criminal justice reform.

The funds provided by Bezos will enable Van Jones and his team to design and implement programs that prioritize rehabilitation, job training, and support services. These initiatives have the potential to transform lives by providing opportunities for education, skill development, and economic stability.

Bezos's contribution highlights the importance of collaborative efforts among philanthropists, activists, and policymakers in effecting meaningful change. By investing in initiatives aimed at reducing recidivism and promoting successful reintegration, Bezos's philanthropy serves as a catalyst for creating a more just and equitable society.

With the tightening of financial resources, there was a significant shift in leadership within the jail's health-care administration. Our longstanding leader, Russell Boley, whose demeanor and character were well-suited to the chaos, controversy, and pressures inherent in the jail environment, retired. He was known for his easy-going nature, which allowed us to carry out our duties without feeling intimidated or burdened by negativity. His presence provided a sense of stability and calmness in an environment already fraught with stress and tension. He understood the value of letting a team function holistically, without the need to micromanage his team.

Navigating the challenges of working in a jail setting is inherently demanding for health-care workers, correctional officers, and inmates alike. Mr. Boley's leadership style, characterized by his ability to alleviate unnecessary pressures and foster a supportive atmosphere, was instrumental in maintaining a semblance of order amid the chaos.

However, with the arrival of new leadership, marked by a changing of the guards, my tenure in the jail system ended abruptly. The transition brought uncertainty and upheaval, signaling a departure from the familiar and a shift toward the unknown for all of us.

My team achieved significant milestones during our time in the jail system. The flourishing jail diversion program, renowned throughout the country, stands as a testament to our collaborative efforts. The improvements made in providing essential mental health support to inmates were the direct result of a cohesive working system comprising jail health-care staff, administrators, and mental health professionals.

Reflecting on our accomplishments, I now understand why great leaders often face detractors. Effecting systemic change requires challenging entrenched ideologies, addressing deep seated fears, and confronting the general apathy toward those who are misunderstood or disliked. This struggle for change is exemplified in the stories of individuals like Malcolm X and Jesus Christ, both of whom faced resistance and hostility in their quests for justice and equality.

It is disheartening to acknowledge that even revered figures like Reverend Dr. Martin Luther King Jr. faced surveillance and harassment from institutions like the FBI. The unjust scrutiny and labeling of a man driven by a desire to do good highlight the systemic injustices that persist in society. My own experiences, such as being barred from entering a system that disproportionately targets and harms Black men, further reveal the challenges faced by those advocating for positive change.

Chapter 13: From Ridicule to Resilience: A Journey Through Mockery and Triumph

In life's grand theater, we often find ourselves cast in roles we never auditioned for, facing an audience that can be both merciless and unkind. Inevitably there will be trials and tribulations in navigating a world where ridicule and laughter are all too common. These experiences serve as a testament to the indomitable human spirit is the capacity to rise above adversity. In hindsight, when I take a closer look at the details of my journey I see a few key gems I would love to share with you.

The Sting of Mockery

From the innocent taunts of childhood to the biting jibes of adulthood, the sting of ridicule leaves wounds that often run deeper than mere words. Laughter, once the soundtrack of innocence, can transform into a weapon, piercing through our defenses and leaving scars that linger long after the echoes fade.

We confront these moments with a mixture of pain and resilience, struggling with the sharp contrast between the laughter around us and the turmoil within. Each jest, each mocking glance, feels like a dagger to the heart, shaking our confidence and testing the very core of our being.

Yet, in the midst of this onslaught, we find an unexpected source of strength—a resilience born from adversity, a defiance forged in the crucible of ridicule. We refuse to be defined by the laughter of others, determined to rise above the hurtful words and judgmental stares.

As we navigate the treacherous waters of ridicule, we discover that our true power lies not in shielding ourselves from laughter, but in our ability to transform it into fuel for growth and self-discovery. We learn to embrace our vulnerabilities, recognizing that they are not signs of weakness but badges of courage in a world that often seeks to tear us down.

And so, we rise, bruised but unbroken, emboldened by the knowledge that laughter may wound but cannot extinguish the light that burns within. For in the face of ridicule, we find our resilience, our strength, and ultimately, our true selves.

The Temptation of Retreat

When faced with ridicule, the instinct to retreat into the shadows can be all-consuming. The relentless laughter and scorn of others can feel like a spotlight shining on our vulnerabilities, urging us to shrink back and conceal our true selves. In those moments, the fear of further mockery and embarrassment looms large, casting a shadow over our confidence and self-assurance.

We confront these moments with a heavy heart, grappling with the internal conflict between authenticity and self-preservation. We are strongly tempted to hide behind masks and facades and to blend into the background to escape the piercing gaze of ridicule. We may question whether it is worth exposing ourselves to the risk of further hurt and humiliation, or whether it is safer to retreat into the safety of anonymity.

Yet, in the depths of our vulnerability, we find a glimmer of courage—a spark of defiance against the forces of ridicule. We realize that hiding our true selves only perpetuates the cycle of shame and self-doubt, reinforcing the notion that our worth is determined by the acceptance of others. We come to understand that true liberation lies not in retreat, but in the bold act of embracing our authenticity, flaws and all.

So, we stand on the precipice, our hearts pounding with fear and uncertainty, yet our spirits are burning with determination. We take a deep breath and step out of the shadows, refusing to let ridicule dictate our worth or define our destiny. In that moment of courage, we reclaim our power and declare to the world that we will not be silenced or diminished by laughter. For it is in the face of ridicule that our true strength is revealed—not in the absence of fear, but in the audacity to confront it head-on, to embrace our vulnerability, and to shine brightly in spite of the darkness.

Embracing Vulnerability

In the rawness of vulnerability, we discover a hidden reservoir of strength waiting to be tapped. It is in those moments of openness and authenticity that we unlock the transformative power of embracing our vulnerabilities.

In a world where ridicule lurks around every corner, daring to be authentic is an act of defiance—a refusal to conform to the expectations of others, regardless of the consequences. It is a declaration of self-worth, a tribute to our inherent value as individuals deserving of respect and acceptance.

Though the risk of ridicule may loom large, we refuse to let fear dictate our actions. Instead, we choose courage—the courage to stand tall in the face of laughter, to own our imperfections, and to embrace the full spectrum of our humanity.

For it is in embracing our vulnerabilities that we discover our true strength. It is in acknowledging our flaws and insecurities that we cultivate resilience, empathy, and compassion—for ourselves and for others.

And so, we dare to be vulnerable. We dare to show up, to speak out, and to live authentically, knowing that the journey may be fraught with challenges but also have moments of profound growth and self-discovery.

In vulnerability we find liberation. Liberation from the constraints of judgment and expectation, and liberation to live our lives on our own terms, guided by the light of our own truth.

My Detour Felt Like a Dead End
The diversion from Miami-Dade County jail felt like encountering a dead end. The sudden, compelled departure, marred by accusations and misunderstanding, left me feeling isolated and disheartened. It disrupted the course I had set out on, acting as a significant obstacle to my pursuit of meaningful change and advocacy. Though I wished to remain, the grip of political forces and the jail system's control prevented me from doing so.

Leaving the Miami-Dade County jail amid accusations of demeaning an inmate was a bitter and deeply unsettling experience. The weight of humiliation and embarrassment bore down heavily on me, particularly as someone who holds the dignity of every individual in the highest regard. To be accused of such misconduct cut to the core of my principles and values.

In that moment of uncertainty and doubt, I contended with feelings of frustration and disillusionment. The setback seemed insurmountable, casting a shadow of doubt over my purpose and convictions. Questions swirled in my mind, echoing the whispers of self-doubt and apprehension.

Yet, even in the midst of darkness, a flicker of hope remained. I drew strength from my faith, my family, the stock from which I came, allowing me to channel the resilience of my ancestors, who faced far greater challenges with steady resolve. Their indomitable spirit served as a guiding light, illuminating the path forward through the shadows and trenches of adversity.

Slowly but surely, I began to reclaim my sense of purpose and direction. I refused to let this detour define me or derail my commitment to justice and equality. Instead, I embraced it as a necessary pause, a moment of reflection and introspection on the journey toward greater understanding and compassion.

As the fog lifted and clarity emerged, I realized that this detour was not a dead end, but merely a temporary divergence from the main road. It was a chance to recalibrate, to reassess my priorities and reaffirm my dedication to the causes that matter most.

In retrospect, I see now that this detour was a valuable chapter in my journey, shaping me in ways I could never have anticipated or imagined. I indeed did not know it all; who knew? I can now smile on this lesson as it taught me resilience in the face of adversity, humility in the midst of uncertainty, and the firm conviction to stand up for what is right, even when the path ahead seems uncertain.

Though the road may be long and winding, I am steadfast in my determination to press forward, knowing that every detour, every obstacle, only strengthens my resolve and fuels my passion for creating a brighter, more just world for all.

As a person of color, the ordeal stirred familiar echoes of past injustices and systemic biases. Throughout history, people of color have borne the brunt of insults, negativity, and belittlement, enduring the cruel taunts and ridicule of a society steeped in prejudice. These experiences, though painful, have become an indelible part of our cultural fabric, a reflection of our resilience and strength in the face of adversity.

In grappling with the fallout from these accusations, I couldn't help but recognize the broader societal implications at play. My own experience served as a microcosm of the systemic injustices that pervade our institutions and communities. It revealed the urgent need for greater awareness, empathy, and accountability in confronting and dismantling the deeply entrenched forms of discrimination and oppression that continue to marginalize and disenfranchise.

Despite the personal toll, I resolved to channel my experience into a catalyst for change. I refused to allow myself to be silenced or sidelined by the injustice I had endured. Instead, I committed myself to advocating for meaningful reform and accountability within the criminal justice system, striving to ensure that no one would ever again face the indignity and mistreatment I had suffered.

I carry with me the resilience and determination of generations past, standing firm in the face of adversity and striving to create a more equitable and compassionate world for future generations. Reflecting on my journey, I am reminded of a troubling incident during my residency. One of my medical school classmates recounted how his resident referred to him as his "slave." At the time, there were only four Black students in a class of more than 200. Despite the profound discomfort and offense we felt, the fear of reprisal and the overwhelming sense of isolation prevented us from speaking out or protesting against such degrading treatment.

In the United States, it is distressingly easy for a Black person to be arrested, falsely accused, and even killed before ever reaching a jail cell. The swiftness with which I was removed from a setting that many would deem frightening and horrific continues to astonish me to this day.

Yet, amid the challenges and complexities of working in such an environment, I found solace and purpose in my interactions with the officers responsible for the care, custody, and control of inmates. Despite the inherent difficulties, many of them displayed genuine concern and compassion for those in their charge. It was in these moments of connection and collaboration that I discovered a sense of fulfillment and camaraderie, even as I sought to impart my knowledge and expertise to my fellow residents.

156

I was honored to be selected by the chairperson of the Department of Psychiatry to lead the inaugural forensic training program at the University of Miami Miller School of Medicine. Over the course of my tenure, I had the privilege of training approximately six to eight residents, imparting to them the knowledge and skills necessary for navigating the complex intersection of mental health and the legal system.

However, my time in this role was not without challenges. A subsequent change in the administration of the Department of Psychiatry led to my abrupt removal from the position. Despite this setback, my passion for studying the law remained undiminished.

As a psychiatrist, I am uniquely positioned to evaluate individuals who have become entangled with the legal system. My expertise in understanding human thought processes and behaviors equips me with valuable insights into the complexities of forensic psychiatry. When I explain my profession to children, I often describe myself as a doctor who helps people with problems related to their thoughts and behaviors.

My departure from the jail marked a somber chapter in my life, leaving behind a place that had been a significant part of my journey. However, it was not until the tragic death of an inmate named Randy Heath that I found myself drawn back into the realm of correctional health care.

The circumstances surrounding Heath's death were nothing short of appalling. The images of his emaciated body broadcasted in the media, served as a raw memory of the unfathomable neglect he endured. It is inconceivable that anyone could witness his deteriorating health on a daily basis and fail to intervene in any meaningful way. Such indifference is not only inhumane but also borders on criminal neglect.

During my time at the Miami-Dade County jail, such a tragedy would have been unthinkable. The sense of camaraderie among staff extended beyond professional duties, manifesting in holiday celebrations and shared meals. Even inmates benefited from this camaraderie, with leftovers from staff gatherings often distributed to those who helped maintain cleanliness of the facility.

In stark contrast to Heath's tragic fate, the inmates under our care during my tenure often improved in their health, albeit due to the side effects of medication and limited exercise opportunities. That improvement shows the positive impact that compassionate and attentive health care can have within a correctional environment.

The departure of the jail director and the director of medical services shortly after my own exit marked a significant period of transition for the institution. However, even with new leadership in place, the systemic issues plaguing the jail persisted. In the aftermath of Randy Heath's tragic death, I maintained a vigilant eye on developments in the jail, relying on media reports to stay informed.

Expanding on the situation in the Miami-Dade County jail system as of 2024 it is crucial to investigate the reasons behind the federal scrutiny and ongoing challenges faced by the facility. This could involve examining various factors such as overcrowding, inadequate staffing, insufficient resources for mental health care, and systemic issues contributing to mistreatment or neglect of inmates. Additionally, exploring any recent incidents or controversies could shed further light on the situation.

Regarding the turnover in leadership within the psychiatric department, a deeper analysis could explore the reasons behind the high rate of turnover and its impact on the quality of mental health care. This might involve investigating issues such as burnout among psychiatric staff, organizational culture

158

within the department, challenges in recruitment and retention of qualified professionals, and the effectiveness of succession planning and leadership development initiatives.

Furthermore, examining the broader implications of instability within the psychiatric department, such as its impact on inmate well-being, staff morale, and overall institutional effectiveness, would provide valuable insights. Understanding how turnover in key leadership positions affects the delivery of mental health services and the overall functioning of the jail system is essential for identifying areas for improvement and implementing sustainable solutions.

Chapter 14: Pathways to Improvement: Strategies for Positive Change

In this pivotal chapter, we examine actionable strategies for improvement of the system as a whole. Despite the myriad challenges faced by the institution, there are tangible steps that can be taken to foster positive change and improve outcomes for both inmates and staff.

Patients Not Prisoners

Lisa Taliaferro, is the CEO of the nonprofit, Patients Not Prisoners that works to create solutions for those experiencing mental illness. Her dedication to ensuring that individuals living with mental illness receive proper care instead of being criminalized is beyond commendable. She founded Patients Not Prisoners in Florida to continue her mission of advocating, educating, and supporting the cause.

In the dimly lit corridors of correctional facilities, where freedom is a distant memory, the thin line between punishment and rehabilitation often blurs. Yet, within these walls, the role of healthcare professionals remains clear and unwavering: to provide care with dignity and compassion. Patients, not prisoners, lie behind those steel bars, each one deserving of the same respect and medical attention as any individual in the outside world. Compassionate healthcare in prisons is not merely a moral obligation but a crucial component of holistic rehabilitation. By viewing and treating incarcerated individuals as patients first, healthcare providers can foster a sense of humanity and hope, breaking the cycle of neglect and mistreatment. This approach not only aids in the physical and mental well-being of the incarcerated but also paves the way for a more just and humane society. Embracing this philosophy ensures that the care provided transcends the constraints of confinement, recognizing the intrinsic value of every human life.

Enhancing Mental Health Services

Prioritizing mental health care within the jail system is not just recommended; it is imperative. This involves several key steps to ensure that inmates with mental health issues receive the support and treatment they need:

- Increase Staffing Levels: One of the first steps is to boost the number of mental health professionals. This includes psychiatrists, psychologists, social workers, and psychiatric nurses who are trained to assess and treat mental illness.

- Expand Access to Treatment: In addition to increasing staffing levels, it is crucial to expand access to psychiatric treatment and therapy for inmates. This may involve providing regular counseling sessions, medication management, and access to specialized treatment programs for conditions such as substance abuse or trauma-related disorders.

- Implement Evidence-Based Interventions: It is essential to implement evidence-based interventions that have been proven to be effective in addressing mental health issues in jails. These may include cognitive-behavioral

- therapy, dialectical behavior therapy, and other therapeutic modalities tailored to the unique needs of inmates.

- Provide Comprehensive Care: Mental health care within the jail system should be comprehensive, addressing not only psychiatric symptoms but also the underlying factors contributing to mental illness, such as trauma, substance abuse, and socioeconomic stressors. This may involve collaborating with community resources and organizations to provide holistic support to inmates.

- Ensure Continuity of Care: Finally, there should be a focus on ensuring continuity of care for those transitioning out of the jail system. This may involve developing discharge plans, connecting inmates with community-based mental health services, and providing follow-up support to prevent relapse and re-incarceration.

By prioritizing mental health care within the jail system and implementing these strategies, we can work toward creating a more humane and effective approach to addressing mental illness.

Strengthening Staff Training and Support

Investing in comprehensive training programs for correctional staff is not only crucial but also fundamental for fostering empathy, cultural competence, and effective de-escalation techniques. By providing staff with the necessary tools and skills to understand and address the complex needs of incarcerated individuals, we can create a more supportive and therapeutic environment.

These training programs should cover a range of topics, including mental health awareness, crisis intervention, trauma-informed care, and conflict resolution. By enhancing staff's understanding of mental illness and its impact on behavior, they can better respond to challenging situations with compassion and empathy.

Further, establishing robust support systems for correctional staff is essential for mitigating burnout and promoting overall well-being. Peer counseling programs can provide a valuable outlet for staff to process their experiences, share resources, and seek guidance from colleagues who understand the unique challenges of working in a correctional setting.

Additionally, providing access to mental health resources, such as counseling services and wellness programs, can help staff cope with the stress and emotional toll of their work. By prioritizing staff well-being, we can create a more resilient and compassionate workforce capable of providing high-quality care.

Addressing Overcrowding and Infrastructure

Overcrowding presents a multitude of challenges within the jail system, ranging from substandard living conditions to stretched resources. To address this issue effectively, it is imperative to explore alternatives to traditional incarceration for nonviolent offenders. Diversion programs and pretrial services offer viable solutions that prioritize public safety while alleviating overcrowding pressures.

Diversion programs divert offenders away from the criminal justice system and into community-based interventions, such as substance abuse treatment, mental health counseling, or vocational training. By addressing the root causes of offending behavior, these programs not only reduce recidivism but also ease the burden on overcrowded jail facilities.

Pretrial services, including supervised release and electronic monitoring, allow those awaiting trial to remain in the community under certain conditions rather than being held in jail. This not only helps prevent unnecessary detention but also promotes fairness and equity in the justice system by ensuring that pretrial incarceration is reserved for those who pose a genuine flight risk or threat to public safety.

Investing in infrastructure upgrades and modernization efforts is essential for improving conditions and promoting the well-being of both inmates and staff. This includes renovating facilities to meet safety and sanitation standards, expanding capacity to accommodate growing populations, and incorporating technology to streamline operations and enhance security measures.

164

By implementing these strategies in tandem, jurisdictions can effectively address overcrowding in jails while upholding public safety and ensuring humane treatment.

Promoting Transparency and Accountability

Open communication channels and transparent policies serve as foundational pillars for fostering trust and accountability within correctional institutions. By establishing clear lines of communication among staff, inmates, and external stakeholders, institutions can promote transparency and facilitate the exchange of information.

Regular audits and independent oversight mechanisms play a crucial role in ensuring accountability and identifying areas for improvement. These audits, conducted by impartial third parties or oversight bodies, help assess compliance with established policies, procedures, and standards of care. They provide valuable insights into areas of strength and weakness, enabling administrators to implement targeted interventions and corrective measures.

Community engagement also plays a vital role in promoting transparency and accountability. By actively involving community members, advocacy groups, and other stakeholders in decision-making processes, institutions can enhance public trust and legitimacy. Community input can inform policy development, program implementation, and resource allocation, ensuring that institutional practices align with community values and priorities.

Fostering a culture of accountability requires promoting a sense of responsibility among staff at all levels. Training programs, performance evaluations, and disciplinary measures should emphasize the importance of ethical conduct, adherence to policies, and respect for the rights and dignity of all inmates.

By prioritizing open communication, transparent policies, regular audits, independent oversight, and community engagement, correctional institutions can uphold standards of accountability, promote public trust, and ensure the well-being of both staff and inmates.

Advocating for Policy Change
Meaningful reform demands proactive advocacy efforts at both the local and state levels. Collaborating with a diverse array of community stakeholders, policymakers, and advocacy groups is essential to champion legislative initiatives aimed at addressing systemic issues and implementing changes.

One crucial area of focus is bail reform, which seeks to address disparities in pretrial detention and reduce the reliance on cash bail, which often criminalizes poverty. By advocating for policies that prioritize risk assessment and community-based supervision over monetary bail, stakeholders can work toward a fairer and more equitable pretrial system.

Sentencing reform is another critical aspect of criminal justice reform. Advocating for alternatives to incarceration, such as diversion programs, rehabilitation, and restorative justice initiatives, can help reduce reliance on punitive measures and promote rehabilitation and reintegration.

Additionally, advocating for the expansion of diversion programs can divert individuals away from the criminal justice system and toward community-based treatment and support services. These programs offer alternatives to incarceration for individuals with mental health issues, substance use disorders, and other underlying needs, helping to address root causes of criminal behavior and to reduce recidivism.

By collaborating with community stakeholders, policymakers, and advocacy groups, stakeholders within the Miami-Dade

County jail system can collectively advocate for legislative reforms that prioritize fairness, equity, and compassion.

Together, they can work toward creating a criminal justice system that upholds the rights and dignity of all while promoting public safety and community well-being.

The Prison System's Math Isn't Math'n

The issue of gerrymandering with respect to incarcerated individuals is a significant and often overlooked problem. For years, the Census Bureau has counted incarcerated people based on their place of confinement rather than their true home addresses. This practice inflates the populations of areas with prisons, giving them undue political influence when state and local governments redraw district lines every decade. This flawed method exacerbates racial disparities, undermines democratic principles, and treats incarcerated individuals as mere statistics rather than constituents.

Moreover, this practice contradicts the Census Bureau's own guidelines, as other groups like military personnel, students, and travelers are counted based on their home addresses or places of long-term residence, not temporary locations. The inaccurate counting of incarcerated individuals distorts representation and affects electoral outcomes by artificially boosting the population count in areas with prisons, thereby diluting the voting power of communities outside these districts.

Recognizing these issues, over a dozen states have taken steps to address prison gerrymandering, passing legislation to ensure that incarcerated individuals are counted at their true residential addresses rather than at their places of incarceration. States like Maryland, New York, California, and others have implemented reforms to correct Census data and prevent the distortion of political representation during redistricting processes.

Moving forward, advocates argue for a fairer approach that respects the true residency of incarcerated individuals. Allowing them to declare their own addresses or using Department of Corrections' records for Census purposes could provide a more accurate representation of communities and ensure that every person, regardless of their incarceration status, contributes equitably to the democratic process.

Picking Up the Slack

To further address the root causes of incarceration, there is a pressing need to reevaluate our educational priorities and vocational training opportunities. A return to emphasizing non- technical skills such as construction, plumbing, and electricity in school curricula can provide viable career pathways for young people, particularly those in underserved communities.

Moreover, the proliferation of substandard educational institutions, often referred to as "mom-and-pop schools," must be addressed. These institutions lack essential facilities and resources, contributing to a lack of educational opportunities and exacerbating the pipeline to incarceration.

In addition to educational reform, graduate and professional students possess a unique set of skills and perspectives that can be instrumental in addressing the complex needs of individuals within the jail system. These students, pursuing advanced degrees in fields such as psychology, social work, law, public health, and education, bring specialized knowledge and training to the table, enabling them to offer targeted interventions and support tailored to the diverse needs of incarcerated individuals.

Graduate and professional students can contribute to various aspects of jail reform and rehabilitation efforts. For example, students in psychology and social work can provide mental health services, including counseling and therapy, to inmates struggling with trauma, substance abuse, and other psychological challenges. Through evidence-based interventions, they can help individuals develop coping skills, improve self-esteem, and address underlying issues contributing to their involvement in the criminal justice system.

Similarly, law students can offer legal assistance to inmates, advocating for their rights, facilitating access to justice, and challenging unjust practices such as wrongful convictions and excessive sentencing. They can also work on policy initiatives aimed at reforming the criminal justice system, promoting alternatives to incarceration, and advocating for the rights of marginalized communities disproportionately impacted by mass incarceration.

Public health students can contribute to inmate health and wellness initiatives, addressing issues such as infectious diseases, chronic conditions, and substance use disorders within correctional facilities. By conducting research, implementing prevention programs, and advocating for improved healthcare access, they can help reduce health disparities and promote holistic well-being among incarcerated populations.

Moreover, education students can play a vital role in developing and implementing educational programs within jails, empowering inmates with valuable knowledge and skills to succeed academically and professionally upon reentry into society. By offering literacy programs, vocational training, and GED preparation courses, they can enhance inmates' opportunities for personal growth, economic self-sufficiency, and social integration post-release.

Overall, graduate and professional students have a crucial role to play in advancing jail reform and supporting the rehabilitation and reintegration of incarcerated individuals. Through their expertise, passion, and commitment to social justice, they can contribute to creating a more humane, equitable, and effective criminal justice system that prioritizes rehabilitation, redemption, and second chances for all.

It is imperative to prioritize the mental health and well-being of both inmates and correctional staff. This includes increasing access to mental health professionals, implementing evidence-based interventions, and providing comprehensive training programs for correctional staff to promote empathy and de-escalation techniques.

Expanding diversion programs represents another crucial step in reducing the reliance on incarceration and promoting alternatives to traditional punishment. These programs should be accessible to individuals from all backgrounds and demographics, offering support and resources to address underlying issues such as substance abuse, mental illness, and poverty. By diverting individuals away from the criminal justice system and toward community-based interventions, we can foster rehabilitation and reduce recidivism rates.

Moreover, it is imperative to prioritize the mental health and well-being of both inmates and correctional staff. This includes increasing access to mental health professionals within correctional facilities, implementing evidence-based interventions for treating mental illness, and providing comprehensive training programs for correctional staff to enhance their capacity for empathy and effective communication.

In essence, addressing systemic issues within the criminal justice system requires a multifaceted approach that encompasses education, diversion, and mental health support. By investing in preventative measures and community-based interventions, we can work toward creating a more equitable and humane system that prioritizes rehabilitation and social justice for all.

Addressing issues of overcrowding and infrastructure inadequacies is crucial for improving conditions. Exploring alternatives to incarceration for nonviolent offenders, such as diversion programs and pretrial services, can help alleviate overcrowding while ensuring public safety. Additionally, investing in infrastructure upgrades and modernization efforts can create a safer and more dignified environment for inmates and staff.

Ultimately, fostering a culture of transparency, accountability, and compassion within the jail system requires collaboration and commitment from all stakeholders. By working together to implement evidence-based practices and policies, we can create a more just and humane system that promotes rehabilitation and supports the well-being of all individuals involved.

The primary focus of the hiring process for medical and correctional staff should be on identifying individuals who genuinely prioritize the welfare of others. This emphasis on compassion and concern for fellow human beings is essential for fostering a more humane and equitable jail system. To achieve this goal, it is imperative to start nurturing these qualities early, ideally within our institutions of higher learning. By instilling a deep sense of compassion and empathy in future professionals, we can take significant strides toward creating a system that prioritizes the well-being of all.

There exists a pervasive belief that our current system of incarcerating individuals with mental illness, intellectual disabilities, and substance abuse disorders can and should be reformed. This reform aims to create a more humane and effective environment conducive to treatment and rehabilitation. History has shown us that adopting modern treatment approaches, which consider the underlying biological and chemical factors contributing to behavioral distortions, can lead to positive outcomes for those within the system.
A critical component of improving the system is to implement better recruitment strategies, with a specific focus on attracting

students of color. During my time in psychiatric residency, I witnessed many residency positions going unfilled, resulting in an influx of applications from foreign medical students. Unfortunately, there existed a stigma surrounding these students, unfairly questioning their academic capabilities compared to their American counterparts. This perception has persisted in the field of psychiatry for some time.

By actively recruiting and supporting students of color, we can foster diversity within the mental health and criminal justice systems. This diversity ensures that individuals from marginalized communities have access to culturally competent care, which is essential for effective treatment and rehabilitation. Additionally, by challenging and dismantling stereotypes and biases within the field, we can create a more inclusive and equitable environment for all aspiring mental health professionals, regardless of their background or ethnicity.

Throughout my tenure as a teacher and supervisor, I've had the privilege of encountering students whose caliber and dedication are truly remarkable. Their thirst for knowledge is palpable, akin to a sponge eagerly absorbing water. What strikes me most is their genuine commitment to learning and growth, evident in their deep appreciation and gratitude for new information and clinical experiences. It has been profoundly moving to witness their enthusiasm for psychiatry, as their passion for the discipline serves as a beacon of inspiration.

In my experience, age is no barrier to effective teaching. What truly matters is the instructors' enthusiasm and dedication to their craft. This enthusiasm is particularly crucial for cultivating the next generation of Black and Brown psychiatrists, especially within the challenging context of our jails and prisons. Working closely with students from Caribbean schools has renewed my hope that the mental health crisis within incarcerated populations can be addressed by a new wave of passionate and dedicated psychiatrists of color.

However, realizing this vision requires a fundamental shift in the mindset of jail and health-care administrators. They must be willing to embrace and support aspiring psychiatrists of color, welcoming them into correctional facilities to provide much-needed care, particularly to those from marginalized communities. Eliminating discriminatory practices reminiscent of Jim Crow is paramount if we are to truly liberate the minds of young Black men (and women) and confront the systemic injustices in our judicial system.

At its core, psychiatry demands a lack of prejudice, good judgment, and a deep capacity for empathy. I've had the privilege of mentoring students from diverse backgrounds, including several Black students who have expressed a newfound interest in pursuing psychiatry. Witnessing their passion and potential fills me with hope for the future of mental health care, yet it also underscores the urgent need for systemic change.

Ultimately, it is through the passion and dedication of individuals like my students that meaningful change will be achieved. I hope they will continue to carry the torch of passion and empathy, advocating for those who are often overlooked and marginalized and working tirelessly toward a more just and compassionate society. With their unwavering commitment, perhaps we can finally break through the barriers that have long hindered progress and pave the way for a brighter future for all.

As I reflect on the journey chronicled in these pages, I am reminded of the profound impact that individuals can have when they commit themselves to a cause greater than themselves. The stories shared within these chapters are not just anecdotes; they are testament to the power of passion,

173

empathy, and dedication to creating positive change in our world.

In the face of systemic injustices and entrenched prejudices, the individuals whose narratives grace these pages refused to be daunted. They stood firm in their belief that every person, regardless of background or circumstances, deserves to be treated with dignity and compassion. They recognized that the path to progress is not always easy, but they pressed forward with courage and conviction, undeterred by the obstacles in their way.

As we reach the final pages of this book, let us not simply close its cover and move on. Let us carry with us the lessons learned from these remarkable individuals and gained from my experiences, and let them inspire us to action. Let us commit ourselves to being agents of change in our communities, advocates for those who have been silenced, and champions for justice and equality.

For it is through our collective efforts that we can truly make a difference in the world. It is through our constant commitment to compassion and empathy that we can build a society where every person has the opportunity to thrive. And it is through our determination to never give up, no matter the odds, that we can create a future that is brighter and more just for generations to come.

As we bid farewell to these pages, let us do so with deep gratitude for the stories shared, and for the tireless efforts of those who have sacrificed for the advancement and betterment of their professions. Let us carry forward a renewed sense of purpose and faith in our hearts, inspired by the resilience and dedication of those who have come before us.

With these stories as our guideposts, let us embark on our own journeys, determined to write our own chapters in the ongoing story of humanity. Let us seize each opportunity to make a positive impact, to uplift those in need, and to stand as beacons of compassion and empathy in a world that often feels dark and uncertain.

Together, let us envision a future where compassion reigns supreme, and justice is the cornerstone of our society. Let us work tirelessly toward that vision, knowing that our collective efforts have the power to shape a world that is more just, more equitable, and more compassionate for all. It is imperative that we recognize and uplift those who are at a disadvantage, ensuring that they too have the opportunity to experience the equity that some take for granted.

In this shared pursuit, let us embrace empathy as our guiding principle and solidarity as our driving force. Let us amplify the voices of the marginalized and advocate for their rights with unwavering determination. Let us dismantle the systems of oppression that perpetuate inequality and injustice, replacing them with structures built on fairness, inclusivity, and respect for all individuals.

As we journey forward, let us never lose sight of the humanity that binds us together. Let us celebrate diversity as a source of strength and unity and let us cultivate a culture of empathy and understanding in every facet of our lives. For it is only through our collective commitment to compassion and justice that we can truly create a world where every person is valued, respected, and given the opportunity to thrive.

The majority of Black doctors attended medical school at a predominately Black medical school. Meharry and Howard Medical Schools for a while were the only schools where Black students were allowed to attend. Charles Drew Medical Center, Morehouse School of Medicine, and Xavier University School of Medicine will be the primary schools for future Black psychiatrists.

Indeed, sparking greater interest in psychiatry among our younger colleagues is essential for addressing the pressing mental health needs of our communities. Providing them with access to resources, such as the information contained in these noteworthy books, can offer valuable insights into the field, and inspire a passion for mental health advocacy and care.

Enthusiastic mentoring by psychiatric colleagues can play a crucial role in nurturing the next generation of psychiatrists. By sharing their expertise, experiences, and passion for the field, seasoned professionals can guide and support aspiring psychiatrists on their journey.

The Association of Black Psychiatrists has long been a beacon of advocacy and mentorship in the field of psychiatry. The Association's efforts to support and empower Black mental health professionals are invaluable in addressing the underrepresentation of Black doctors, particularly Black males.

It's concerning that the percentage of Black male doctors has dwindled to levels reminiscent of the mid-1980s. This underscores the urgent need for targeted efforts to increase diversity and representation in medicine, particularly in specialties like psychiatry where cultural competency and understanding are paramount.

By actively engaging and mentoring aspiring psychiatrists, advocating for diversity and inclusion in medical education and training, and supporting organizations like the Association of Black Psychiatrists, we can work toward a future where all communities have access to culturally competent and compassionate mental health care.

Reversing these troubling statistics is critical to improving the conditions within our jails and prisons. The existence of "forgotten floors" reveals the urgent need for reform. These floors represent not only physical spaces but also the neglect and indifference toward the well-being of inmates, particularly those with mental health issues.

Closing these forgotten floors requires a varied approach that addresses the root causes of mass incarceration and prioritizes rehabilitation and reintegration over punitive measures. This includes investing in mental health services, diversion programs, and community-based alternatives to incarceration.

We must educate, advocate and liberate those who suffer from mental illness who are incarcerated in jails and prisons for no reason other than having a behavioral disorder or mental illness. We do not lock up people with heart disease, lung disease or kidney disease or cancer.

We must not give incentives to those organizations that make profits from incarcerating mentally ill individuals. We must invest in programs and organizations that promote release, rehabilitation, education, job training and comprehensive treatment from those who suffer from mental illness and brain disorders. Our jail and prison systems must be privatized for reentry programs, housing programs, transitional programs, and educational programs. This will help in the two to three hundred-million-dollar loss by individuals who have a brain or mental disorder.

In conclusion, the path to reforming our criminal justice system and improving conditions within correctional facilities demands unwavering commitment and decisive action. These efforts cannot be merely aspirational but must be practical steps towards a more just and humane society. They require collaboration among stakeholders, sustained advocacy, and a collective and continuous commitment to uphold the rights and well-being of all individuals involved. Together, we can forge a future where compassion guides policy, justice prevails, and every person has the opportunity to rebuild their lives with dignity and hope.

Let us continue to push boundaries, challenge norms, and champion systemic change. The journey ahead may be challenging, but with perseverance and solidarity, we can pave the way for a criminal justice system that truly serves and supports every member of our community in a truly conclusive manner.

Not All Heroes Wear Capes

Our role models aren't the celebrities we see on screens or stages; they're the remarkable people right in front of us, whose actions and achievements inspire us daily.

To my wife, whose curiosity sparked by my familiarity with each name led to a moment of reflection. The truth is, I didn't just know these names; I lived alongside them, learning from their experiences, and celebrating their achievements. Together, we bore witness to history in the making, each name representing a chapter in our collective journey.

They are more than just names on a list; they are the guiding lights who paved the way for me and countless others to walk through the doors of the University of Miami Miller School of Medicine.

- Former Dean Dr. Bernard Fogel, whose leadership and vision shaped the path forward.
- Dr. Robert Bragg, whose dedication to excellence set a high standard for us all.
- Dr. Vincent Ziboh, whose research lab provided invaluable experience during summers spent learning and growing.
- Dr. George L. Saunders, the trailblazer whose footsteps we followed as the first Black graduate.
- Dr. Elwood McGhee, whose mentorship and support were instrumental in my journey to medical school.
- Dr. William Luckey, whose skill and compassion marked the beginning of my journey into parenthood.
- Dr. Earl Allen, whose expertise and wisdom guided us through challenging times.
- Dr. Asa Yancey, a pioneer in psychiatry training at UM/JMH Medical Center, whose achievements paved the way for future generations.

- Dr. Anthony Nealy, Dr. Matthew Rose, and Dr. Farley Neasman, whose dedication to their craft inspired us to excel.
- Dr. Cornelius James Jr., a product of our community whose success reminded us of the importance of representation.
- Dr. Frederick Bloom, Dr. Herman Miller, and Dr. Rodney Young, whose contributions to medicine left an indelible mark.
- Dr. Douglas Nalls, a steadfast friend and colleague who shared the journey with me.
- Dr. Jacqueline Simmons, a trailblazer who shattered barriers as the first black female graduate.
- Dr. Carey Green, Dr. John McAdory, Dr. Thomas Garvin, Dr. Dollie Green, Dr. Shaun Hoyes, Dr. Gerald Leggett, Dr. John O Brown, Dr. William Patterson, Dr. Dazelle Simpson, and Dr. George Simpson, your enormous achievements continue to inspire and motivate us.

These individuals aren't just names on a page; they are the embodiment of resilience, determination, and excellence. They are the reason we strive to make a difference every day.

"Reclaiming The Narrative" by Deanna Pierce, 2024

Epilogue

Reflecting on the changes in the Miami-Dade County jail system since my time there, I'm humbled to see progress. In the past, our small team of four psychiatrists cared for a larger inmate population. With thirteen psychiatrists now overseeing a diminished inmate population, the system has indeed seen some changes, but there's still a considerable distance to cover before reaching its full potential.

Remarkable improvements have taken place with the establishment of a state-of-the-art facility, replacing the older one where I once provided care for mentally ill inmates awaiting trial. This progress owes much to the dedication of many.

Moreover, Miami-Dade County's creation of a Behavioral Health Advisory Board demonstrates a commitment to addressing mental health issues. It's my sincere hope that this board represents our diverse population and appoints individuals who truly understand our community's needs.

Looking ahead, I wonder who will step up and take charge in the same way as the many whose dedication to mental health advocacy has made a profound impact. Their legacy serves as a reminder of the importance of continued progress in fostering a more compassionate society.

About Dr. Joseph Poitier, M.D.

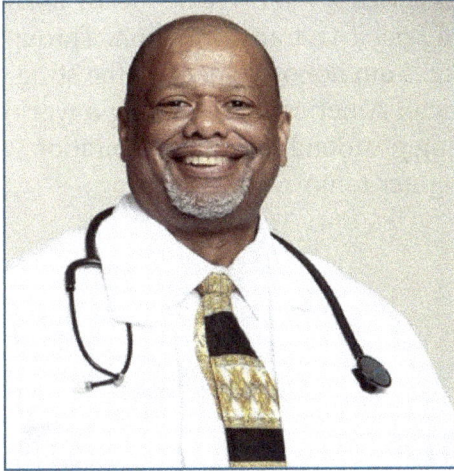

As a seasoned psychiatrist based in Miami, Florida, boasting over forty-three years of dedicated service in the medical field, my journey has been defined by resilience, tenacity, and an unwavering commitment to helping others. Motivated by a desire to enact change, I pursued a career in medicine, earning my medical degree from the University of Miami Miller School of Medicine in 1980. Throughout my rather fulfilling career, I have tirelessly devoted myself to providing compassionate care to underserved populations, particularly those grappling with mental illness within the criminal justice system.

I grew up in a family with deep roots in the Bahamas, and I have faced the harsh realities of systemic racism and socioeconomic disparities from an early age. Yet, it was these very challenges that fueled my determination and ignited my passion for advocating for marginalized communities.

Beyond my professional achievements, my most covenanted achievement has been my gift to serve as a devoted family man and recognition as an esteemed community leader. I draw inspiration from my upbringing and cultural heritage,

leveraging my experiences to drive advocacy and activism aimed at fostering positive transformation. Through my insightful writing, I am honored to share the struggles and triumphs of African Americans navigating a world marked by adversity, offering profound insights, inspiration, and a beacon of hope for a brighter tomorrow.

"The Why, The Mission" by Deanna Pierce, 2024

About Deanna Pierce

Also born and raised in Miami, Florida, my journey has unfolded across diverse sectors. One chapter in my journey stands out—the chapter of my tenure at the Department of Youth Rehabilitation Services (DYRS) in Washington, D.C., where I served as the Director for the Office of Internal Integrity. DYRS, entrusted with the guidance and care of youths navigating the rocky terrain of delinquency, mirrors a reality fraught with challenges akin to its adult counterparts. Over time, the veil lifted, revealing a truth both sobering and profound—juvenile corrections, once perceived as transformative, often served as a mere stopgap, perpetuating cycles of despair, particularly among marginalized communities. This is precisely why community development organizations like the Overtown Youth Center, which provides a set of comprehensive programs and services for youth, adults, and families in our community, are so critical. Founded in 2003 by NBA Hall-of-Famer Alonzo Mourning and real estate developer Martin Z. Margulies in the hope of creating a safe haven for children living in Overtown and neighboring communities, the center has filled a tremendous void in our community by delivering high-quality services through a framework designed to bridge educational, social, emotional, health, and economic gaps.

What began as an optimistic view of juvenile corrections as a transformative opportunity for youth to redirect their lives quickly evolved into the sobering realization that the system often served as a mere transition rather than a true transformation. Seemingly enough, the juvenile corrections system and the adult corrections system both proved to connect minorities synonymously with a habitual cycle where those who were in need most often did not get the care they so desperately needed. Access to meaningful and impactful resources is paramount.

For instance, an imprudent mental health professional may exhibit poor ethics, weak boundaries, and questionable therapeutic skills, potentially aggravating rather than alleviating an individual's symptoms. This can lead to wasted time and resources, lack of progress toward goals, potential emotional distress, and in extreme cases, harm. It may also negatively impact one's trust in seeking help again and hinder opportunities for personal growth. Conversely, great mental health care providers embody kindness, respect, and effective intervention strategies, guided by robust ethical principles.

In pivotal fields such as therapy, where misguided "guidance" can prove detrimental, it's imperative for individuals to access trustworthy and skilled professionals who not only hold qualified credentials but also possess a genuine passion for their work. This dedication makes all the difference. That's precisely why professionals like Dr. Poitier, Dr. Klifton Fehr, and countless others are so effective—they have demonstrated the aptitude to truly transform lives and cultivate meaningful change. They understand the assignment at hand and approach their professional duties with a high level of seriousness and responsibility. My personal journey has taught me the valuable lesson that some individuals are irreplaceable due to their unmatched passion and unwavering commitment to their craft.

189

From a rather deep and personal unspoken introspection (for a few notable reasons), I know for certain I would have ended up in very different circumstances, akin to those I encountered within the system's confines. If you know anyone born or raised in Miami, you know that we have a culture of often bragging and boasting about being "born and raised in the County of Dade" or being from "the 305"—long before Rick Ross, Flo Rida, DJ Khaled and Pitbull made us a familiar hashtag. I can attest that these heartfelt sentiments have been truly earned, and we wear them like a badge of honor, with good reason. However, these earned stripes have come at a cost, often bittersweet and sometimes tinged with traces of survivor's remorse, imposter syndrome, an array of embedded trauma, and triggers that many of us have paid for—with interest, often resulting in enduring consequences.

If you are a minority born in Miami-Dade County, you likely have stories and memories of those less fortunate who fell victim to the city's perils. The success stories that bring me the greatest joy are those of Ryan Hawkins, President & CEO of the Jessie Trice Community Health System; Coop (DC), who keeps us safe in the shadows; and Winston Lee, the founder of Cuffed Design, Inc. These men grew up in Miami and overcame significant challenges to achieve remarkable success. I often keep them and their families in my prayers. The fact that they attended Florida A&M University makes me smile even more.

In the vibrant tapestry of Miami, where pride in roots runs deep, I have witnessed a symphony of survival marked by tales of loss and resilience. These stories stand in stark contrast to my early education at The Cushman School. Notice I said "started," because I am most certainly a byproduct of Miami-Dade County Public Schools. I applaud my parents' belief that a great education alone was insufficient; social adaptation and balance were also crucial, and I experienced the extremes of both contrasting worlds.

190

The stories of our hometown comrades, etched in our memories, serve as nostalgic reminders of the fragility of life. You never really forget certain people whose memories are ingrained in you and have shaped your past. I still have many of their obituaries in my office desk, not just to preserve their memory, but as a continual reminder that my love and hate relationship with this city runs much deeper than most. Living in this city has toughened many of us, becoming a defensive mechanism that molded us into the persons we needed to be for survival. However, this adaptation comes at a price over time. While maybe essential for immediate safety at some point, it isn't conducive to anyone's long-term health and well-being.

I find great joy in observing individuals who have found their path to peace and are either addressing or have addressed their past traumas. What brings me even greater joy is witnessing the remarkable progress of those committed to the entire process of becoming the best versions of themselves, embracing courage as they undergo unique transformations. The true mode in which humans flourish is one of resilience, where we confront challenges while also prioritizing our mental, emotional, and physical well-being.

In previous iterations of myself, I felt the need to be *tough* and outspoken to garner respect, influenced by past traumas and triggers. The loss of any loved one is inherently traumatic, but losing a father can be particularly profound for daughters. Such a loss can evoke a complex mix of emotions and healing from such a loss is a non-linear process. Personally, I am deeply grateful for the support of men among men like Fred Alderman, Maurice Bryant, Mike Preston, and Henry Lee Jefferson, who stepped in to fill the void left by my father's absence during various pivotal times in my life. Their presence and support have been invaluable in navigating such a profound loss.

Now, with a shifted perspective, I recognize the profound impact of trusting in God's guidance. It enables me to embrace a gentler manner, speaking with a softer voice, while remaining authentic to who I am. This invaluable insight has been a blessing when least expected. Amid life's trials and tribulations, I find solace in a select few entrusted loved ones and the divine providence that guides our steps. I am eternally grateful to those who, through their actions rather than mere words, stand and have stood steadfastly by my side, being intentional, weathering life's storms with me and equally sharing in life's joys.

I thank Father Alexander Ekechukwu, C.S.Sp., for giving me the gift of perspective rooted in spiritual wisdom and understanding of life's challenges and triumphs. Through his insightful teachings and altruistic pastoral care, he has provided me with a fresh vantage point to see beyond immediate circumstances, learning to embrace those who see me, to be amiable to those who don't, fostering a deeper understanding of spiritual truths, and the broader meaning of life.

I extend my heartfelt gratitude to my godparents, whose unwavering support and guidance have been immeasurable. Their love, wisdom, and encouragement have profoundly shaped who I am today. Their presence has been a constant source of strength and comfort, and I am eternally grateful for their enduring faith in me. Thank you for your remarkable influence and for being such an integral part of my journey.

The "invisible protections" I attribute to my blessings haven't come about purely by chance. These days, I find myself embracing gratitude for the twists and turns, the victories and the defeats, for all that unfolded differently than I imagined or planned. I know that in the grand design, God's wisdom reigns supreme as my creator. I am thankful to God for not giving me what I wholeheartedly thought was meant for me and for removing such things I was settling for from my life in His

own way. I am listening now, you have my ear, I promise :)
Thy will be done.

God's protection and favor, along with my village of loved ones, has amounted to nothing short of pure deliverance. How great is God that protects us even when we may not know him or care to know him as he knows us? He loves us without fail, even when we may not know him at all. His mercies remain constant, even when our faith and belief may falter, stray, or even be delayed. I am not oblivious to these facts, and I am thankful that he does not keep score because I could never repay or balance the ledger of such acts of benevolence.

Most importantly, this work is dedicated to the resolute spirit of my beloved mother and the cherished memory of my late father. Before there was a "Roman Pope," there was my father who, as only he could, never failed to encapsulate society's pressure on and expectations for Black women, emphasizing the importance of class, intelligence, and beauty in navigating the world. His lessons remain meaningful, and his wisdom echoes within me. To my mother who is as unique as her name, whose beauty has always shone brightly in my heart: your endless love and tireless sacrifices have illuminated my path, revealing the true essence of beauty and strength. In your selflessness, you've shown me that being "enough" is not measured by outward standards, but by the depth of one's character and the warmth of one's heart.

As a woman still figuring it out and finding the late-blossoming joy in it all, my parents' guidance has been my beacon through life's challenges. In humble gratitude, I dedicate this book to the enduring legacy you both have created for me. Your love, wisdom, and support continue to inspire me every day, I thank you for the blessing of coming from good stock and being nurtured by such remarkable individuals.

I can assure you that I had no intention of being an author, by no means. However, I am learning to laugh at my plan versus His plans. As Proverbs 19:21 says, 'Many are the plans in a person's heart, but it is the Lord's purpose that prevails.' I thank the Poitier family for their persuasion to be a part of something so beautiful, special, and well-timed.